TEACHER

Bible Readers Series

A Study of Revelation

HOPE
FOR THE
FUTURE

Evelyn Laycock

Abingdon Press / Nashville

Hope for the Future
A Study of Revelation

Copyright © 1997 by Cokesbury.

Revised edition Copyright © 2000 by Abingdon Press.

Scripture quotations in this publication, unless otherwise indicated, are from the New Revised Standard Version of the Bible copyrighted © 1989 by the Division of Christian Education of the National Council of the Churches of Christ in the United States of America, and are used by permission.

Lessons are based on the International Sunday School Lessons for Christian Teaching, copyright © 1993, by the Committee on the Uniform Series.

ISBN 0-687-09131-4

00 01 02 03 04 05 06 07 08 09—10 9 8 7 6 5 4 3 2 1
Manufactured in the United States of America.

CONTENTS

THE TIMELESSNESS OF APOCALYPTIC LITERATURE

By Jim Durlesser

A grotesque red dragon with ten horns on its head glares at me menacingly. It rises from the sea; and as it churns the water with its massive body, lightning comes down from heaven and strikes the earth. Fortunately, the great red dragon is glaring at me only from a brochure that is on my desk as I write this. I—along with most other people in my area who can be identified for postal purposes as "Resident"—recently received the brochure. It advertises a lecture series called "The Time of the Beast."

As I open the brochure, I see another picture of the great red dragon rising out of the sea. Lightning bolts still flash from the sky. In this picture, however, the great red dragon is accompanied by a lion with wings, a bear with tusks, and a leopard that has four heads and four wings. The brochure invites people to attend a seminar in order to understand biblical prophecy, the Book of Revelation, and the beast. Recipients of the brochure are also invited to learn eight ways to identify the Antichrist.

The seminar that this brochure is advertising reflects the fascination that people have with apocalyptic literature. Our fascination with this literature is understandable. The bizarre symbolic images are captivating. The narrative patterns found in many apocalyptic works make exciting stories. And, of course, there is the belief that the secrets of the future are to be found in apocalyptic literature—if only the reader can crack the code of symbols. Our society, like many before us, is concerned about the future. We want to know where we are headed.

Perhaps most significantly, however, apocalyptic literature speaks to us of the ongoing struggle between good and evil. Will evil destroy us? Or, will good vanquish evil in the end? Will we have to suffer? Or, will we be miraculously delivered from evil's worst assaults?

I believe that human interest in the answers to these questions about the ongoing struggle between good and evil is what bestows a certain timelessness on apocalyptic literature. Beyond the popular fascination with the symbols in apocalyptic literature, beyond the glossy brochure promising understanding of the Book of Revelation and ways to identify the Antichrist, beyond the futile attempts to set up a calendar of the "end time," this aspect of apocalyptic literature spans the generations. Reaching back across the centuries to the birth of apocalypticism during the era of the Babylonian Exile, the timelessness of apocalyptic literature is rooted in its bold affirmation that, regardless of how powerful evil may seem, good will be victorious in the end.

Apocalypticism germinated in this period of suffering and exile (the sixth century B.C.); began to blossom in a time of disillusionment, political turmoil, and economic hardship (late sixth century B.C. to early fifth century B.C.); and gradually came to full flower in an era of political oppression and religious persecution (first half of the second century B.C.). As people continued to experience alienation, economic and physical persecution, oppression, and even threat of death, apocalyptic literature flourished during the last centuries B.C. and the first centuries A.D. Perhaps the apocalyptic hope that God will vanquish evil is timeless because suffering and the experience of evil are timeless. The Book of Daniel, set in the time of the persecution of Jews during the Babylonian Exile, was written in response to the wicked policies Antiochus Epiphanes pursued between 167 B.C. and 164 B.C. The Book of Revelation, recalling the terrible persecution of Christians in the A.D. 60's by the Emperor Nero, was probably written during the time of persecution in the A.D. 90's by the Emperor Domitian. The message of the Book of Daniel is that there have been and will be other leaders like Antiochus. The message of the Book of Revelation is that there will be other leaders like Nero and Domitian.

AN EXAMPLE OF TIMELESSNESS

A close look at Revelation 13 will help us explore the timelessness of apocalyptic literature. As the chapter opens, the satanic dragon stands along the seashore (Revelation 2:18). Then, two beasts rise up—the first out of the sea (13:1), the second out of the earth (13:11). The first beast, who is given power and authority by the dragon (13:2), represents Rome and the Roman Empire, which, at the time John received his revelation, Christians thought were the earthly incarnation of the Antichrist. We know that the first beast represents Rome because of an interpretation of the beast given in Revelation 17.

In Revelation 17, John sees a "great whore." In verses 1 through 6, he describes her in disgusting detail. Notice that in verse 3, the "great whore" is said to be "sitting on a scarlet beast that was full of blasphemous names, and it had seven heads and ten horns." This beast, full of blasphemous names and with seven heads and ten horns, is the same beast as the one that rises up in Revelation 13, that John describes as "having ten horns and seven heads ... and on its heads were blasphemous names" (3:1). Revelation 17:9-10 explains the beast's seven heads on which "were blasphemous names." In these verses, an angel tells John that "the seven heads are seven mountains on which the woman is seated." What city is built on "seven mountains" or seven hills? Rome!

The angel goes on to explain to John that the seven heads also represent seven kings and in Revelation 17:11 comments that an eighth head/king is expected, which "belongs to the seven." So, the angel is talking about seven, and then eight, of the emperors of the Rome Empire.

Verse 6 of Revelation 13 reports that the beast "opened its mouth to utter blasphemies against God," cursing the divine name and dwelling. The Roman emperor, from the time of Julius Caesar on, was deified. Temples were built and dedicated to the emperors, and the emperors were worshiped as gods. Domitian, who was emperor at the time John received the revelation, required his subjects to call him "our lord and god." Such were the "blasphemies" uttered by

the beast—claims of divinity, claims to be lord, claims to be god, claims of power that no human should make.

The second beast, the beast that rises out of the earth in Revelation 13:11, "exercises all the authority of the first beast on its behalf, and it makes the earth and its inhabitants worship the first beast" (13:12). So, while the first beast represents Rome, the Roman Empire, the emperor, and the emperor cult, the second beast represents the officials of Rome scattered throughout the Empire who carry out the blasphemous, wicked policies of the emperor.

John observes in Revelation 3:11 that the second beast has "two horns like a lamb" but speaks "like a dragon." The second beast, the local officials who force people to worship the emperor, is deceptive. The local officials appear harmless, gentle, and compassionate, perhaps, and from the Christian perspective, even messianic, "like a lamb" (13:11). The words they speak, however, are from the "dragon" himself. The local officials who carry out the policies of the wicked Roman Empire seem harmless enough, but they are agents of the evil side. Indeed, the second beast is extremely dangerous; for he is given the authority to order that "those who [will] not worship the ... [first] beast ... be killed" (13:15).

The Roman Empire minted coins that bore the image of the reigning emperor and his titles, some of which were claims of deity. Across the Empire, all business had to be carried out using the currency of the Empire. John is probably talking about such coins when he speaks of "the mark" of the beast that one has to possess in order to "buy or sell" (Revelation 13:17).

For a Christian to oppose the "beast," for a Christian to refuse to worship the emperor and to acclaim the emperor as "lord and god," for a Christian to refuse to use coinage that bore an image of the emperor and referred to the emperor in divine titles, meant economic repression, if not physical persecution and martyrdom. People had to possess and use the "mark" of the beast in order to "buy or sell." References to having the mark on "the right hand or the forehead" (Revelation 13:16) are probably symbolic, like much of the imagery in the Book of Revelation that we have been discussing.

John indicates that this "mark," the image, is "the name of the beast or the number of its name" (Revelation 13:17). This number, John says, "is the number of a person" (13:18). It is the famous six hundred sixty-six.

In the ancient world the written letters of the alphabet were frequently also used for numbers. This was the case in both Hebrew and Greek. People often added the value assigned to the letters of the name and came up with "the number of [their] name" (Revelation 13:17). Can we use this method to determine whose name totals six hundred sixty-six?

Many different possibilities have been suggested for the identity of this person. Most likely, however, this person is the wicked emperor Nero, the emperor who reigned from A.D. 54 to A.D. 68 and who ordered the martyrdom of so many Christians. According to church tradition, Peter and Paul were both martyred in Rome during the reign of Nero.

How would the numerical value of Nero's name total six hundred sixty-six? In Hebrew, the alphabet on which the six hundred sixty-six is probably based, the name *Nero Caesar* is spelled N R W N Q S R (Hebrew has no vowels in its alphabet, only consonants.). The letters of Nero's name in Hebrew and their numerical values are as follows:

$$N \quad R \quad W \quad N \quad Q \quad S \quad R$$
$$50 + 200 + 6 + 50 + 100 + 60 + 200 = 666$$

What then is the message of Revelation 13? What is John's revelation regarding the dragon, the two beasts, and the name with the triple sixes? What do we learn from this chapter about the timelessness of apocalyptic literature?

First, John is saying that the Emperor Nero and presumably all others like him will always be shy of perfection. In biblical numerology, *seven* symbolizes perfection, completeness, totality. *Six* is one less than *seven*. So, by saying that the emperor is six six six, John is saying that, as hard as the emperor tries, he will never be "seven." He can claim divinity all he wants. He can force people to worship him as a god. He can have temples dedicated to him all over the Empire. But he will never *really* be a god. He will always come up short of true perfection, true completeness, true divinity. In short, the emperor will never be seven seven seven.

Second, John is cautioning all who read the Book of Revelation to beware of leaders who claim powers for themselves that they have no business claiming. Such leaders appear to be one thing, "lamblike," when they are really something quite different, "dragonlike." John warns us about following these deceptive leaders, who seek to abuse their power by drawing us and our allegiance away from the God of biblical faith and toward them.

Third, John is urging us to be watchful of leaders who use economic and political power to persecute others and to ruin peoples' lives. Persons who are willing to compromise their principles and to obtain the "mark of the beast" will be fine and will probably even flourish. Those who refuse to "wear the mark of the beast" will face severe persecution, however.

Thus, when we view the contents of Revelation 13 and the rest of the Book of Revelation in their historical context and seek to understand the meaning of the imagery contained in John's vision in light of what was going on when he received the revelation, we find far more than events that some people think will fit into a calendar of happenings sometime in the future. Rather, what we find are profound warnings of a timeless quality—warnings against leaders who oppress their people through economic means; warnings against leaders who claim power for themselves that they have no business claiming; warnings against leaders who insist that their people offer them complete obedience, devotion, and service; warnings against leaders who engage in brutal torture of their people if they refuse such obedience and service. In short, John is telling his readers that leaders like Nero and Domitian can arise at any time, so be forewarned.

TIMELESS APPLICATIONS

When I taught a study of the Book of Revelation, I was intrigued by the timelessness of the applications that people found in John's vision of the dragon and the beasts. Some students made immediate comparisons between the Roman emperors and Hitler, the "Fuhrer," the "Leader"—the claims of power, the persecution, the deaths that were ordered for all who resisted.

Other students applied John's timeless warnings in the Book of Revelation to the tyrannical, oppressive policies that affected the lives of the people of the former Soviet Union and the Soviet bloc in Eastern Europe. One of my students pointed out that the Soviet Union promoted an almost religious view of the state and its founders. Other students reminded the class of the violent repression of dissent in the countries of the Soviet bloc in Eastern Europe.

When I was teaching this study of the Book of Revelation, Haiti's military regime was collapsing. Some of my students compared the Roman emperors to Lieutenant General Raoul Cedras, the leader of the military-backed government that oppressed Haiti for years and pursued policies leading to the torture and death of any who dared to oppose the regime.

As the discussion in class continued, students applied John's timeless warnings to the business and industrial world as well, where, when dealing with some powerful multinational corporations, if you expect to "buy or sell," you are forced to "wear the mark" of the corporation. That is, you are expected to cooperate with the company, to behave in a certain way, to believe certain things, to affirm certain loyalties, and to carry out certain services. Some class members shared personal stories of how they or family members had been persecuted by leaders of corporations who perceived themselves to be godlike; how they or family members had lost their jobs, been passed over for a raise, or been "blackballed" because they refused to compromise their Christian principles and beliefs and do as the company demanded.

One student brought John's timeless warnings home to our group in an intriguing way by pointing out that we do not need to go to other countries or other periods of history to find leaders who abuse their power and institute policies that destroy the lives of people. All we have to do is look at the politics of some of our cities and towns: "If you play by my rules, you'll get the contract. If you support me, I'll support you. If you don't play by my rules and support me, you'll never work in this town again. You'll never get another contract around here."

Local politics can sometimes get quite dirty. One person, in a quest for godlike power, may begin a smear campaign against an opponent. In the process, the leader who is on a quest for power will destroy the opponent's business, family life, and means of financial security. When this happens, the leader who is abusing power in a quest for godlike status is falling into the six, six, six, syndrome.

Of course, there are countless other applications of John's timeless warnings to his readers to be alert to Nero-like and Domitian-like rulers, to leaders who view themselves as godlike, abuse their power, demand unquestioning obedience from their underlings, and punish severely those who dare to question their authority. Across the centuries, across the earth, Nero-like and Domitian-like tyrants have oppressed their people. Suffering at the hands of such leaders is an unfortunate reality of life that has contributed to the timeless appeal of apocalyptic literature. People who are suffering, people whose lives are in danger from oppressive tyrants, people whose lives are being ruined by the economic policies of power hungry officials— such people can immediately relate to the social setting that produced biblical apocalyptic literature.

TIMELESS APOCALYPTIC HOPE

Beyond the frightening timeless apocalyptic warning against deceptive, tyrannical leaders who are the personification of evil and who are out to destroy all that is good, however, is a comforting timeless apocalyptic hope. This hope affirms that, although evil seems powerful and has brought great suffering and

death to the earth, God ultimately will vanquish evil and bring deliverance to the people of God.

Shortly after the Book of Daniel was written (between 167 B.C. and 164 B.C.), a tiny community of people struggling to be faithful to God established a community on the shores of the Dead Sea and committed their beliefs to writing in what we know as the Dead Sea Scrolls. The people of the Dead Sea community had experienced the depths of evil. Now, all they had to hold on to was the timeless affirmation that, although the powers of evil seem strong and the people of God are faced with terrible opposition and persecution, God will ultimately vanquish evil and deliver the people of God from suffering, oppression, and even death.

Probably the best-known example of apocalyptic literature from the Dead Sea Scrolls is a work known as "The War of the Children of Light and the Children of Darkness" or, more simply, "The War Scroll." The title of the scroll makes clear its topic. Employing "light" and "darkness" as symbols for good and evil, the War Scroll details the preparations by the Children of Light for their war against the Children of Darkness. The text describes the trumpets, the standards, the weapons that will be used, the layout of the camp, and even the prayer that is supposed to be recited when the battle is won. The War Scroll concludes with a description of the battle itself. The first column of the War Scroll affirms the timeless apocalyptic hope that iniquity shall be vanquished, leaving no remnant; "[for the sons] of darkness there shall be no escape. [The sons of righteous]ness shall shine over all the ends of the earth; they shall go on shining until all the seasons of darkness are consumed and, at the season appointed by God, His exalted greatness shall shine eternally to the peace, blessing, glory, joy, and long life of all the sons of light."[1]

Twenty centuries ago this tiny community of God's "Children of Light" who lived along the shores of the Dead Sea affirmed God's sovereign power in the universe over even the most powerful forces of evil. We, as God's contemporary "Children of Light," affirm that, although wickedness seems strong, God is stronger and in the end will be victorious. Popular culture even affirms this point in television, cinema, and fantasy literature. Think of the old Westerns. Who wins? It is always "the good guy," the cowboy in the white hat. Think of George Lucas's *Star Wars* movie. "The Force," the power of good, defeats the evil empire and the personification of evil, Darth Vader. Yet, just when we think that good has won out over evil, the second movie is released; and *The Empire Strikes Back.* In the third film, however, "The Force" is victorious; and good ultimately triumphs over evil.

So, our modern world, especially the modern community of God's "Children of Light," joins the "Children of Light" of the Dead Sea community in seeking to be faithful to God in a time of severe persecution and oppression. Since Old Testament times; since the "Children of Light" of the Dead Sea Community voiced in their scrolls their hopes for deliverance from a corrupt, oppressive world; and since the New Testament period when John received his revelation, countless other "Children of Light" have suffered as the oppressed of society. They have suffered economic, physical, or emotional persecution because of their faith and have longed for deliverance from their plight.

"Children of Light" across the centuries have held courageously to their beliefs in spite of torture and threat of martyrdom. They have held firm to the timeless hope of their apocalyptic literature that even as they were faithful to almighty God, almighty God would be faithful to them. They have held firm to the hope that when the good overpowers the evil in the great and climactic battle, they will be among the righteous who will receive their reward.

[1]From "The War Rule," in *The Dead Sea Scrolls in English,* by Geza Vermes (Sheffield Academic Press LTD, 1987); page 105. The words within the brackets reflect places where the readings are uncertain due to damage to the scrolls.

Chapter One

AVAILABLE FOR SERVICE

PURPOSE

To illustrate ways God's vision is revealed to us through people

BIBLE PASSAGE

Revelation 1:4-15
Background: Revelation 1

> ### CORE VERSE
> Write in a book what you see and send it to the seven churches. (Revelation 1:11)

GET READY

■ Bring to the session a large map that shows the island of Patmos and the seven cities in which the churches to whom Revelation was originally written were located. Notice that if you travel from Ephesus to the other churches and back to Ephesus, you make a circle.

Prior to the session write the definitions of *apocalyptic literature* and *eschatology* (see below) on a chalkboard or large piece of paper. Post the definitions in the classroom for the remainder of the study.

BIBLE BACKGROUND

■ The Book of Revelation is written in a language form called apocalyptic. This word is difficult to define, since it has been used so broadly in our day. In mainly Jewish and Christian literature, apocalyptic or apocalypticism may be defined as the "eschatological belief that the power of evil (Satan), who is now in control of this temporal and hopelessly evil age of human history in which the righteous are afflicted by his demonic and human agents, is soon to be overcome and his evil rule ended by the direct intervention of God, who is the power of good, and who thereupon will create an entirely new, perfect, and eternal age under his immediate control for the everlasting enjoyment of his righteous followers from among the living and the 'resurrected dead.' "[1] Note that the word *eschatological* is used in this definition. *Eschatology* is the branch of theology that is concerned with death, the end of the present age, and life in the age to come. Hence, apocalyptic writing is always eschatological.

The Book of Revelation is said to be the finest example of an apocalypse in existence. This form of writing occurs in times of persecution, when people are facing the possibility of imminent death. Such was the situation in Asia Minor for the early Christians. As the student book states, Domitian was the Roman emperor at the time of the writing. He decreed that being a Christian was a criminal act punishable by death. The Romans confiscated the property and possessions of Christians, leaving the surviving family destitute. In this world of chaos God revealed to John a message for God's people, a message that communicated hope and the assurance that faithfulness to God in their circumstances would result in everlasting life in God's ultimate kingdom.

The visions of Revelation, although confusing to us, are expressed in images that were familiar to the people of John's day. It should also be said that the writer was thoroughly acquainted with the Old Testament and quoted frequently from it. Many Christians in Asia Minor had a background in Judaism. They knew these references, and they spoke anew to the people.

Revelation 1:4. This verse contains the typical form for first-century letter writing. Early in the body of the letter, the writer is identified and the recipient is named. Here we see the name *John* without any other identification. In Paul's letters we find, "Paul, the apostle . . ."; but we have no such claim here. It is believed that John was well known by the seven congregations to which he wrote; therefore, no additional information was needed. The seven churches were in Asia. (In the New Testament, Asia is never a continent; it is a Roman province.) We might ask, Why these seven churches? There is speculation that these seven were experiencing more intense persecution than others. Still another possibility is that at one time the churches could have been under the writer's authority. The fact is, we simply do not know why these seven churches were addressed.

Grace and peace are offered to the churches by God, who is changeless and eternal, and by the seven spirits. These spirits are mentioned in many places in Revelation. They appear to be a combination of Jewish angels (messengers of God) and heavenly bodies that have some power over what is to happen on earth.

Verse 5a. A third source of grace and peace is Jesus Christ. Three titles are ascribed to Jesus:

(1) **The faithful witness.** A witness is one who speaks from firsthand knowledge. Jesus is the unique person with such knowledge of God's actions.

(2) **The firstborn of the dead.** This is a reference to the Resurrection. Also, included in this title is a Jewish tradition that the firstborn son inherited his father's honor and power.

(3) **The ruler of the kings of the earth.** Two important concepts are found here. First, Psalm 89:27 states, "I will make him the firstborn, / the highest of the kings of the earth." Jewish scholars maintained this verse was a description of the coming Messiah. Thus, making this statement about Jesus was making a claim for his messiahship. Second, when Jesus was tempted by the devil, Jesus was taken up on a high mountain and shown all the kingdoms of earth and their glory. The devil said, "To you I will give their glory and all this authority; for it has been given over to me, and I give it to anyone I please. If you, then, will worship me, it will all be yours"

(Luke 4:6-7). The devil was bargaining with something that was not his. Instead, the suffering on the cross and the power of the Resurrection gave Jesus Christ his universal lordship. He is the ruler of the kings of the earth.

Verse 5b. John used the present tense when he said Jesus loves us, which indicates a present ongoing relationship. Jesus freed us (past tense, act completed) from our sins (separation from God) by his blood. Jesus' sacrifice on the cross was an act in history that is a continuous expression of God's love for humankind.

Verse 6. Jesus' sacrifice made it possible for us to have citizenship in the kingdom of God. In addition, his sacrifice made us priests. In the Jewish tradition only the priests had access to God. Through Christ access to the presence of God is now open to every person. So glory and dominion belong to Christ forever.

Verse 7. John was living in a time when being a Christian was dangerous. The best way to keep courage alive was to remember the faithfulness of God. John did this by expressing confidence in the triumphant return of Christ, which would release the Christian from persecution and domination. He said the day would come when those who killed Jesus would look on him again, for he is the one who is Lord of the universe. But the text goes even further: All people who sin will wail when Christ returns.

The exclamation that ends the verse is made up of two words—one Greek, the other Hebrew. Both stand for a solemn affirmation: "So it is to be. Amen." Using both languages underlines the certainty of the coming.

Verse 8. Here is a tremendous description of God. *Alpha* is the first letter in the Greek alphabet; *Omega* is the last. Writing in this manner indicates the completeness of God. In addition, God is eternal—"who is and who was and who is to come." A third characteristic of God is that God is almighty; God has dominion over all things. The circumstances in which John wrote called for this description. The Emperor was considered to be almighty. Here, however, John reminds the church that only God is truly almighty; and as long as the church is faithful, the church will not be destroyed.

Verse 9. This verse allows us to know more about John. He introduces himself, not by a title, but by a relationship—brother. He has shared and is sharing the persecution with the people of the churches and knows firsthand what they are experiencing. John is on Patmos, a barren, rocky island ten miles long and six miles wide. He was banished there—a common form of Roman punishment—for his faith in Jesus.

Verse 10. Here we have a passage of great historical significance; it is the first reference in literature to the Lord's day. We know from other writings that the observance of the Lord's day began in Asia Minor. The Christian church ceased to observe the sabbath and instead worshiped on Sunday, for the Lord's day commemorates the resurrection of Jesus Christ on a Sunday.

John was in the spirit, lifted up from space and time into "at-one-ment" with God. John heard a voice like a trumpet. The voice—that of Christ—was a clarion call on John's life and work. He was to become a messenger to Christ's people at one of the most difficult times in the life of the church.

Verse 11. John's message was to go to the seven churches whose names are listed. It has been observed that when a line is traced on a map from Ephesus through the six other cities and back to Ephesus, a circle is formed. Some people suggest that since the circle is a symbol of completeness, it may be that the Book of Revelation is for all churches, the complete church.

Verse 12. When John turned to see who was speaking to him, he saw seven golden lampstands. References to lampstands are found in the Old Testament—in the Tabernacle (Exodus 25:31-40), in Solomon's Temple (1 Kings 7:48-50), and in Zechariah's vision (Zechariah 4:2). The lampstands symbolize the fact that John's vision had roots in Old Testament places where God had given revelations.

Verse 13. In the midst of the lampstands John saw one like the Son of Man, dressed in a long robe with a golden sash across his chest. This description of the dress of the glorified Christ is almost exactly like that of the Jewish priests. As previously mentioned, the Jews believed that only the priests had access to God. Here Jesus is seen in his priestly role, one who has direct access to God.

The robe and sash were also the dress of kings and other royalty. Christ is now priest; Christ is now king!

Verses 14-15. Here we have the picture of the risen Christ. However, in describing his features, John again uses Old Testament references.

"His head and his hair were white as white wool, white as snow" (Daniel 7:9)—the preexistent and sinless Christ.

"His eyes were like a flame of fire" (Daniel 10:6). In my office I have a picture of Jesus that helps me understand this description. The eyes of Jesus are so central that they burn into your soul. You immediately feel Jesus knows you, for he really sees you and penetrates your world. In those eyes you see love, caring, joy, sorrow, and friendship.

"His feet were like burnished bronze, refined as in a furnace" (Ezekiel 1:7; Daniel 10:6). The burnished bronze depicts strength and stability that come from being refined in a furnace.

"His voice was like the sound of many waters" (Ezekiel 43:2). In the Book of Ezekiel, the prophet uses these words to describe the voice of God; and John hears Christ speak with the same sound of rushing waters.[2]

INTRODUCE OUR NEED

■ On a lovely fall day in 1990, I had the opportunity to leave a ship and spend part of the day on the island of Patmos. It was Sunday when I visited, the same day of the week that the revelation came to John. As we approached the cave where tradition says John received his revelation, we heard singing coming from the opening. The hymn tune was familiar, but the words were in an unfamiliar language. Arriving at the mouth of the cave, we realized a service of worship was just beginning.

We were cordially invited to join in worship with the congregation. We had to stand for the service because of the size of the cave, yet no one seemed to mind. The service was in the Greek language; but the Holy Spirit bridged the language barrier, and we worshiped in spirit and in truth.

During worship it was possible to visualize John receiving and possibly writing about his revelation in this cave. I could imagine John sending the letter we know as the Book of Revelation to the churches and people whom he knew and loved. It was a holy time, for I became aware at a deeper level how God calls messengers to deliver messages that meet human needs in all times and places.

The student book says that Revelation was written "to speak to a church that needed reassurance in words that would clearly communicate God's care for its future" [page 10]. Ask: *"What parts of the Book of Revelation have you found comforting? What parts have you found disturbing?"* [student book; page 10].

LESSON PLAN

■ The Book of Revelation is as relevant today as it was in the time it was written. Granted, we do not have to be concerned about being burned to death for being a Christian or have to worry about being placed in an arena where there are lions. Yet we do have real issues that seek to destroy individuals and the church. Let us look at the themes in evidence in our Bible Lesson that speak to us in our present circumstances.

(1) Wherever there is a human need, God calls people like John to meet that need. God's nature is to call, to empower, to send. Moses was called to lead the Hebrews out of Egypt. Jeremiah was called to warn Judah that the nation was on a collision course and should repent and return to God. John the Baptist was called to be a forerunner of Jesus. Martin Luther was called to challenge the church on interpretation of Scripture. John Wesley was called to spread scriptural holiness throughout the land. Martin Luther King, Jr., was called to challenge the evil of segregation. Mother Teresa was called to care for the poor and dying in India. Billy Graham is called to preach Christ and to call people to accept Christ as Lord and Savior. God's message and messenger find ways to reach the human heart in every age. Ask: *Which other people can you name who responded to God's call and who became spokespersons for the Kingdom in their time? When have you experienced God's call on your life to be a messenger for him?*

(2) No matter what the circumstances are, God calls us to be faithful. I can imagine how easy it would have been to surrender the Christian faith in order not to experience pain, rejection, and death. The Book of Revelation makes it quite clear that Jesus, too, had experienced these things and knows well these feelings. However, it was because of his faithfulness unto death that the power of the Resurrection was released. Hence, Jesus Christ is the role model for every generation.

In thinking about the horrible persecutions Christians experienced in the first century and some are experiencing now, my friend Minnie Koets, who lives in Amsterdam, Holland, came to mind. I asked her to tell me about the time of persecution she lived through during the invasion of Holland by the Germans during World War II. Here is a portion of the letter she wrote in response to my request:

It started with the invasion of our country on May 10, 1940. No declaration of war, nothing of that, just brutal invasion. First we were dazed and bewildered, then started some fury about the injustice. A powerful fury we thought first, but that changed to stubbornness. Is there really nothing we can do about this? It started slowly the feeling of unity of the Dutch people. Differences fell away, no rich or poor, old or young, etc. We were all together against the enemy. One of the things we did was trying to ignore them entirely, if possible. All over the country people would turn road markings, even took them away. Not that that helped a long time, but you "did" something. . . . When you had washing on the line, you tried to put it like this something red, something white, something blue, the colors of our flag. We would like to have put out our flag, but you could be shot or put in a concentration camp.

As you can tell from Minnie's writing, English is not her first language; but hers is a powerful witness to the creativity and ingenuity of the human spirit. The soldiers with all their weapons could not conquer the mind and soul of the Dutch people. Ask: *What is the message in this letter for us and for the church?*

(3) The power of God is alive in the person of Jesus. The titles listed and the names given in our Bible Lesson tell us immediately who Jesus is. Jesus came to our world, learned our language, suffered pain like ours, and experienced temptations as we do in order to teach us God's language, enable us to know God's nature, and lead us in doing God's will.

Many Christians were concerned in 1996 when three major magazines had pictures of Jesus on the front cover with articles inside questioning the authenticity of the Resurrection. This kind of debate has been around for many years and will probably continue for many more, but the comments were quite disturbing. For John, the question of the identity of Jesus was settled; the Jesus of history is the resurrected Lord. Ask: *Who is Jesus to you? What names, words, or titles would you use to describe Jesus?*

(4) The mission and work of the church is to carry on the mission and work of Jesus. The power to carry out this mission comes from God, Christ, and the Holy Spirit. The church is not the creation of humans; it is God's creation, and it will stand forever. In the Book of Revelation, we see the promise and jubilation that the church will experience in its final triumph. We find the affirmation that Christ does have the final victory. The student book states, "Hopefully, we will be glad we are a part of it, discovering with the early Christians that though the church has its imperfections, it is still God's way of continuing the ministry of Jesus Christ and preparing persons for an eternal future" [page 13]. Ask: *In what ways is our church carrying on the work of Christ?*

(5) The events described in the book will occur very soon. The Book of Revelation is apocalyptic writing, which means it focuses on what will happen at the end of the age and beyond. The book indicates that the events described in John's vision will take place shortly:

"what must soon take place" (1:1)
"for the time is near" (1:3)
"See, I am coming soon!" (22:7)

"Do not seal up the words of the prophecy of this book, for the time is near" (22:10)

"The one who testifies to these things says, 'Surely I am coming soon' " (22:20)

As yet, the end of the age anticipated in Revelation has not come. Through the centuries people have used the book to identify certain leaders and events on the world scene. Kaiser Wilhelm of Germany, Benito Mussolini, Adolph Hitler, Joseph Stalin, and Fidel Castro have all been identified as the Antichrist. The "mark of the beast" has been identified as Social Security numbers and the Universal Product Code. Books have been written about the various interpretations of the number 666.

Although the specific events in Revelation have not yet occurred as described, the great eternal truths in the book have spoken and will speak to every age.

The first of these truths is that God will ultimately triumph over evil. The resurrection of Jesus Christ is evidence of that truth. Any evil is temporary, for evil has built into it its own seed of destruction. This is a given in creation; history is a record of this truth. The fall of Rome was inevitable, the destruction of the Berlin Wall predictable; evil will not triumph. This timeless truth gives strength and motivation in difficult times.

A second eternal truth found in the Book of Revelation is that, no matter what takes place in life and in death, God will take care of those who are faithful to him. In life the Christian is not exempt from pain, sorrow, and tragedy; but he or she has the presence and power of God in and through these experiences. In death, the Christian is released from a body that has many limitations to the Kingdom that God has prepared—the kingdom of God's eternal reign.

The Book of Revelation is a message of hope to the faithful in Christ. What a difference it makes to know that good always triumphs over evil. Evil never wins! And, no matter what takes place in life, God is with us.

Therefore, the ultimate question is not, When will the end of the age come? The most important question is, Am I now open to receive God's kingdom and its resources and to live in the blessed assurance that in life and in death I am in the love of God?

To close the session, pray the prayer at the end of the lesson in the student book [page 13].

[1] From *The Interpreter's Bible*, Volume XII (Abingdon Press, 1957); page 347.
[2] Information on verses 4–15 in this section drawn from *The Revelation of John*, Volume 1, by William Barclay (The Westminster Press, 1976); pages 32–53.

TRY ANOTHER METHOD

■ Apocalyptic writing uses words with hidden meanings. The Book of Revelation has many code numbers, such as 666, 7, and 10, and phrases like "a time and times, and half a time." There may be people in your class or in your church who can share experiences they have had in using similar code words or numbers (a ham radio operator, someone who has been in the armed forces, or a computer operator).

One example: A magazine called *73* began arriving at our home. I had no idea what this title meant; but one of our sons, a ham radio operator, knew immediately; it meant "Hello!"

An article in the newspaper told how prisoners of war in Korea used taps on the wall for letters of the alphabet. You may have veterans in your congregation who could relate their experience of communicating in such a time.

Chapter Two

CALLED TO BE FAITHFUL

PURPOSE

To encourage us to remain steadfast when confronted by forces that oppose our faith

BIBLE PASSAGE

Revelation 2:8-17

> **CORE VERSE**
> Be faithful until death, and I will give you the crown of life. (Revelation 2:10)

GET READY

■ If your classroom has a worship center, place such objects as a baseball, a diploma, a business or professional license, a picture of a house, a family portrait, a picture of a church, a designer shoe, or some money on the center. Or, you may place the objects on a card table brought for the occasion. Use the objects at the designated time in the session to illustrate what some of our cultural faith centers are. Ask members of the class if any of these objects have been or are a center for them and what additional items they might add to the group.

Display a map of Asia Minor if available.

If you plan to use the first optional method, contact class members early in the week.

BIBLE BACKGROUND

■ Our Bible Lesson from Revelation 2 begins with the letter to the church at Smyrna. Smyrna was thirty-five miles north of Ephesus and had the reputation of being the loveliest city in Asia. Located strategically at the end of the road that crossed Lydia and Phrygia and went on to the Far East, Smyrna enjoyed the trade of the rich Hermus valley. The letter reveals that John knew the city well and cared deeply for the church there.

Revelation 2:8. The letter to the church at Smyrna is the shortest of the seven messages and has no condemnation—only commendation—for the church. John addresses the letter "to the angel of the church." The student book says that the meaning of the word *angel* is "messenger." This term might also mean the pastor or some other leader of the congregation. Or perhaps, in light of the usage of the word *angel* elsewhere in the Book of Revelation, it could refer to the spiritual guardian angel of the church.

The letter opens with the resounding titles of the One who is giving the revelation: "These are the words of the first and the last, who was dead and came to life." The phrase "the first and the last," here speaking of Christ, is directly related to an Old Testament title given to God:

> Thus says the LORD, the King of Israel,
> and his Redeemer, the Lord of hosts;
> I am the first and I am the last;
> besides me there is no god.
>
> (Isaiah 44:6)

The next phrase, "who was dead and came to life," says Jesus was dead, something that happened and has now passed; but he also "came to life," a reference to the Resurrection. Jesus Christ experienced death but came to life again and is alive now and forevermore.

Verse 9. The risen Christ was aware that the Christians in Smyrna were having to endure persecution and poverty. The persecution was no doubt the result of refusing to take part in emperor worship. Even though it was at times illegal to be a Christian, persecution for this "crime" was not continuous in Smyrna; but it could break out at any moment.

Poverty was a way of life for the Christians for two reasons. First, most Christians came from the lower classes of society; and the gulf between the rich and the poor was wide. Also, it was not unusual for people or mobs to attack and destroy the homes of Christians, plunder their goods, and leave them with nothing but life itself. Ask: *Are there any similarities to this kind of persecution in our day? If so, what are they?*

Following the mention of their poverty, the risen Christ then adds, "even though you are rich." These words are a reminder that riches are not made up of possessions and safety but come from a vital relationship with Christ—something that can never be destroyed or taken away.

From the letter we see that some Jews in Smyrna were also contributors to the persecution of the Christians. They were falsely accusing the Christians of being agitators against the civil authorities. Christ tells the Smyrnan Christians that these people are not true Jews but are controlled by Satan.

Verse 10. We find in this verse a belief that Christians will experience suffering; it can be expected. Some will be thrown in prison for ten days and be tested. Imprisonment was certainly not what we think of today; it was a prelude to death. The reference to ten days is not to be taken literally; it is an apocalyptic expression for a short time that will come to an end. Christians are to be faithful in such situations. If they are, they will receive "the crown of life."

Verse 11. Here is another promise for those who remain faithful: "Whoever conquers will not be harmed by the second death." The phrase "the second death" occurs in the New Testament only in the Book of Revelation (2:11; 20:6, 14; 21:8). The origin of this phrase may be in Judaism. Some Jews taught that there are two deaths—the physical death that all people will experience and a spiritual death into which the wicked will go after they die ("the lake of fire"). The faithful will not be harmed by this second death.

Verse 12. We now turn to the letter to the church in Pergamum, a city about fifty miles north of Smyrna.

This city claimed many distinctions:

(1) Historically, it was the greatest city in Asia; it had been a capital city for almost four hundred years.

(2) Its geographical position made the city quite impressive. It was built on a conical hill that dominated the valley of the River Caicus.

(3) Pergamum was renowned for its library, which contained approximately 200,000 parchment rolls.

(4) Pergamum was a great religious center, having two famous shrines—one to Zeus and the second to Asklepios. The shrine of Zeus came about as a result of the city winning a victory against the Gauls in about 240 B.C. To commemorate this victory, a great altar to Zeus was built in front of the temple of Athena. The altar stood on a huge platform surrounded by colonnades. It is said to have looked exactly like a throne. On this altar animal sacrifices were burned twenty-four hours a day.

Pergamum was also connected with the worship of Asklepios, the god of healing. The Sanatoria attached to the temples of Asklepios were the forerunners of modern hospitals. The sick and lame were laid there in the hope that one of the sacred snakes would touch them and heal them.

(5) Pergamum was also the center for the worship of the Roman emperor in the province. This was the one religion that covered the whole Roman Empire. Once a year everyone had to appear before a magistrate to burn a pinch of incense to the godhead of Caesar and say, "Caesar is Lord."

We may seem to have spent a lot of time describing the city of Pergamum, and we have. But in order to understand the letter, we need to understand the city, its culture, and its problems. John knew the city and its people well, and he wrote from that background.

The letter is addressed to "the angel of the church in Pergamum." The contents are from the risen Christ who has the sharp two-edged sword. Roman governors were divided into two categories—those who had the sword and those who did not. The ones who had the sword had the right to sentence people to death and therefore had the power of life and death over them. The proconsul who had headquarters at Pergamum had the right of the sword; but the letter reminds the church that it is Christ, not the proconsul, who has the sharp two-edged sword. The power of Rome cannot match the power of the risen Lord.

Verses 13-17. The risen Christ says to the congregation at Pergamum, "I know where you are living." Pergamum was not an easy place for Christians to live, for this was where Satan's throne was—a probable reference to Caesar worship as mentioned in the student book [page 18]. However, some scholars believe Satan's throne also included the altar of Zeus and the worship of Asklepios. Hostility to the church was more intense and more vicious in Pergamum than in most other places. In spite of these circumstances, the church was faithful. The believers held steady and were a vital force even though Antipas, a faithful Christian witness, was put to death in order to persuade the Christians to forsake their faith and to discourage others from becoming Christians.

Even though most people were faithful in this church, others were not. Major problems existed within the church. The Christians were facing enemies without and enemies within. Some persons in the church held to the teaching of Balaam and the doctrine of the Nicolaitans [Nik-uh-LAY-uh-tuhns]. The student book states that this group believed they had found a new freedom in Christ that gave them license to do anything they wished morally and economically. They ate meat that had been sacrificed to idols, and they indulged in sex outside of marriage. This group had adopted a lifestyle similar to that of the people around them and expected God to endorse it. They sought to persuade Christians that there is nothing wrong with conforming to the world's standards, and they encouraged others to join them in doing so.

Ask: *Can you think of some areas in which conforming to the world's standards is a problem in today's church? If so, what are they?* (*Class members may mention gambling, adultery, the abuse of alcohol and other drugs, sexual abuse, power struggles in the workplace, and so forth.*)

The risen Christ invites such persons to repent because there is a Christian morality, a Christian lifestyle, that is expected and must never be compromised. If these people do not repent, Christ will make war against them with his sword. Ask the question on page 19 in the student book: *"What do you believe is required to restore people to full communion with God and/or the Christian community?"*

We need to listen, really listen, to what the Spirit is saying to the churches. All of us know it is possible to listen at different levels. One way is to let it "come in one ear and go out the other"; or we can listen at a literal level, nothing more. But here the church is being asked to listen with the head, with the heart (the home of all emotions), and with the soul to what the risen Christ is saying. For those who do listen, there are rewards.

The first reward is "hidden manna" (Revelation 2:17b). This is clearly a reference to the manna God gave to the children of Israel when they were wandering in the wilderness (Exodus 16). But what does the word *manna* refer to in apocalyptic writing? Three concepts come to mind:

(1) To the Jews, "to eat the hidden manna" meant to participate in the messianic age. For the Christian, it could mean to receive the blessings of the kingdom of God now and to expect to live in the future Kingdom when the new world arrived.

(2) Or, the hidden manna may mean to eat heavenly food. On earth, the Christians could not eat at tables where heathen customs were observed; but they will fully participate in the heavenly banquet of the coming Kingdom.

(3) Another concept is that manna is the bread of God given to humankind through the Lord's Supper. Jesus said, "I am the bread of life. Whoever comes to me will never be hungry" (John 6:35). If the hidden manna and the bread of life are the same, then the manna represents Christ himself given to those who are faithful.

A second reward is a white stone with a new name on it that no one knows except the one who receives it. In the ancient world one of the commonest of all customs was to carry an amulet or charm. A white stone was greatly prized, especially if it had the name of a god on it. To know a god's name was to have a certain power over the god and to be able to solicit aid from this god when needed. The student book says that the "white stone" was the way prisoners were informed they had been found innocent. In light of these traditions the risen Christ seems to be saying, "The white stone you will receive signifies your salvation and my presence with you in life and in death, for I am (my name is) the true and living God."[1]

INTRODUCE OUR NEED

■ The title of our lesson, "Called to Be Faithful," is a powerful phrase. In every age and in all people, we see God seeking to meet human needs through faithful witnesses. Witnesses come in all sizes, nationalities, ages, and educational and economic levels. They are found in homes, schools, streets, churches, factories, office buildings. This fact was illustrated when I was invited to be in leadership in The School of Prayer at a large inner city church.

When I arrived, the pastor told me this church had intentionally chosen to stay downtown instead of moving to the suburbs because such a move would say to the people of the area that they were not important to God or to the church. The pastor then said, "I want you to walk with me the eleven blocks of the inner city—to see it, feel it, smell it—in order to know something about the neighborhood we serve." I saw pawn shops, taverns, seedy housing, stores in which most people would not want to shop, and all the other elements that often go with the inner city. As we passed each building, the pastor said, "People in my church pray daily for persons who come here and for the owners of this property. Their prayer is, 'How can we be your witness to them, O Lord?' "

The people we met along the way called the pastor by his first name, not by his title. I asked, "How do these people know you so well?" I'll never forget his response: "Because my laypeople and I are on these streets every day in person and in prayer."

When we arrived at a school, the pastor said, "We have 'drive-by pray-ers.' They are members of the congregation who drive by the four sides of this school every day and pray for the students, faculty, and administrators who are within this building. This is our school; these are our kids; we care about them."

As a result of such prayers, the church has many members who are tutors at the school. Every classroom has homeroom parents from First Church. Members of the church give a party once a month in every classroom. Bulletin boards are attractively decorated twice a month, each with a message of encouragement and hope. Businesspeople in the church visit the school and talk with the students about work—how to establish a business, how to be a good employee or employer, and how to find a job. Lawyers speak about justice issues. Other persons talk about *when* (not *if*) you go to college and discuss what is required to get a scholarship and how to apply.

Is it any wonder that when Sunday morning arrived, people filled the sanctuary during both worship services—including chairs being brought in until the fire code limit was reached? The overflow then went to the fellowship hall to listen to the service through loudspeakers. Is it any wonder that crime has dropped significantly, that the dropout rate in school has diminished, that there is community pride and fellowship, that there are signs of joy?

Let me be quite candid with you: I went to that church to teach in The School of Prayer, but I was taught about prayer through the lives of the congregation and its pastor.

Just as John was called to be a faithful witness through the writing of Revelation, we too are called to be faithful messengers where we are, in the everydayness of life, and with our God-given abilities. God empowers and blesses these efforts. Ask: *How is the faithfulness of our church in evidence?*

■ We use the words *faith* and *faithfulness* often, but do we really understand what is being said? First, let us look at the word *faith*.

Christian faith is a process of investing trust (what you let your whole being rest on) and loyalty (what you are totally committed to) in the kingdom of God so that God's kingdom is lived reality now and in the future. When we place our faith in the kingdom of God, we have inexhaustible resources that will always be available to us and that will never be depleted. When speaking to the Samaritan woman, Jesus said, "Everyone who drinks of this water will be thirsty again, but those who drink of the water that I will give them will never be thirsty. The water that I will give will become in them a spring of water gushing up to eternal life" (John 4:13-14).

When we have faith, our trust and loyalty are centered in the kingdom of God. When we have other centers, we are not in Christian faith. Those in Pergamum who followed the teaching of the Nicolaitans had rejected the kingdom of God and had adopted a lifestyle that was quite similar to that of the people around them. The risen Christ told the Christians in Pergamum that the road they were on leads to death, in spite of the fact that society may say it is acceptable.

I was on my way to lead a spiritual life retreat. To reach the lovely retreat setting, I flew to Nashville, picked up a rental car, and drove for approximately ninety minutes. The radio was already on in the car with country music the order of the day. I halfway listened as songs talked about wives and husbands leaving home, dogs dying, people losing their jobs, and so forth; but then a song caught my full attention. The words were, "Peel me a 'nanner and toss me a peanut, for you sure made a monkey out of me."

I thought, *Christians should sing that song to society.* All around us we hear promises that life will have meaning if we buy a certain brand of jeans, jewelry, shoes, car, deodorant, and so forth. We try these products, only to find that the promises are not true. We are told that education, money, and a job with a fancy title will bring happiness, only to be left empty. Through these painful and costly experiences, we can now sing to society, "Peel me a 'nanner and toss me a peanut, for you sure made a monkey out of me." What we have been told is not true. (Call attention to the worship center display and discuss the suggested questions at this point in the session.)

The similarities between the church at Pergamum

and the twenty-first-century American church are many. We feel external pulls from society. We feel internal pulls to have other centers of faith—such as consumerism, institutions, education, careers; the list goes on and on. We listen and follow, only to end up with a meaningless existence. How relevant are the words, "Let anyone who has an ear listen to what the Spirit is saying to the churches" (Revelation 3:14).

The question then becomes, What is my faith center? If we have Christian faith, the response will be, "The kingdom of God revealed in Jesus Christ."

Turn to the section in the student book entitled "Lessons for the Churches: Faithfulness" [pages 19]. Note that the writer says, "At all times and in all places, faithfulness is basic." Faithfulness is the key to being Christian. Faithfulness does not depend on circumstances, the calendar, other people, our feelings, or our needs. Faithfulness is the essence of the Christian life, for it is present in all times and circumstances.

Sometimes we confuse faithfulness with being busy. Doesn't society say that having a full calendar means you are important? At other times we confuse faithfulness with holding positions of leadership in the church. Aren't titles a measure of our faithfulness? Then there are times when we think faithfulness is giving money so that we can have power in decision making. After all, doesn't the person who gives the most have the right to have his or her own way when decisions are made in the church? Or we confuse faithfulness with faithfully doing Bible study, prayer, and other spiritual disciplines even though our heart is not in them.

Rather, faithfulness to Christ is first an "inside job." Being faithful means having complete trust in and loyalty to Christ, the one who embodied and taught about God's kingdom. Christ's example of love is the guide for faithfulness. The student book states, "When we fail to hold love as the chief cornerstone of Christian interpersonal relations or place our trust in possessions and status instead of in the indwelling Christ, we can easily become dead to him" [page 21].

When love is our nature, we are faithful to prayer and Bible study, not as a duty to "get done" or in order to look religious, but because we yearn for them just as we yearn for food when we are hungry. We give generously of our money, time, talents, and service from a heart filled with gratitude for God's goodness to us, not to control or use others or to have a good reputation. Faithfulness becomes a way of living.

Faithfulness, then, is placing our whole selves in trust and commitment to Christ in order that we grow daily in loving God, loving neighbor, and loving self. As all this is lived out, God's kingdom does come, God's will is done on earth as it is in heaven.

To close the session, sing or read in unison "Jesus Shall Reign." Then pray the prayer on page 22 of the student book.

[1] Information on verses 12–17 drawn from *The Revelation of John*, Volume 1, by William Barclay (The Westminster Press, 1976); pages 87–97.

TRY ANOTHER METHOD

■ Ask several class members in advance of the session to be prepared to present a three-minute talk on each of the following topics:

(1) What types of persecution is the American church facing today?
(2) What are some forms of persecution Christians outside the United States are experiencing?
(3) What does it mean for this class to be faithful to Christ?

Form several small groups. Give each group the following issues for discussion:

(1) How have you experienced persecution for being a Christian?
(2) Read the parable of the good Samaritan (Luke 10:25-37) and/or the parable of the Pharisee and the tax collector (Luke 18:9-14). Discuss each person in the parable(s) in light of the statement, We can be religious and not be Christian.

Chapter Three

HOLD TO SOUND TEACHING!

PURPOSE

To emphasize that sin carries the seeds of its own destruction

BIBLE PASSAGE

Revelation 2:18-29

> **CORE VERSE**
>
> All the churches will know that I am the one who searches minds and hearts, and I will give to each of you as your works deserve. (Revelation 2:23)

GET READY

As you read through newspapers and magazines, clip articles that illustrate how false teaching is making news and shaping lives. National examples that all will remember are David Koresh and the Branch Davidians and Jim Jones and the mass suicide that took place in British Guyana.

Have on hand a map of Asia Minor.

Review the optional methods so you can make any necessary preparations prior to the session.

BIBLE BACKGROUND

■ Thyatira was a great commercial city located southeast of Pergamum on the road that went from Pergamum to Sardis and on to Philadelphia and Laodicea. This was the imperial mail route. (Point out these places on a map.) We know less about Thyatira than we do about the other seven cities mentioned in Revelation 2–3, but some important facts are known.

The student book mentions the numerous trade guilds that were in the city. These were associations for mutual profit, fellowship, and pleasure for artisans employed in the same trade. These guilds were the base for the work and social life of the people, including the Christians.

Thyatira had no special religious significance as did Pergamum, having only a fortunetelling shrine presided over by a female oracle. There is no evidence to show that persecution of Christians was taking place in Thyatira, that is to say, persecution from the Roman government.

The letter to Thyatira is the longest of the seven letters to the churches in Revelation. Of all the letters it is the most puzzling because we have so little definite information about Thyatira. Nonetheless, the study of the words of the risen Christ to the church there has much to say to us, as it did to those to whom the letter was originally written.

Revelation 2:18. The letter is addressed, as are the previous letters, to the "angel of the church." The message comes from the Son of God, a title Jesus used to express his relationship with God. The Son of God has eyes like a flame of fire and feet like burnished bronze. This description repeats one of an angelic messenger given in Daniel 10:6: "His body was like beryl, his face like lightning, his eyes like flaming torches, his arms and legs like the gleam of burnished bronze." (This imagery is also found in Revelation 1:14b-15.) A familiar expression is, "The eyes are the window of the soul." The "deep things of Satan" (Revelation 2:24) taking place in the church angered the soul of Jesus. The description of the Son of God in this verse aptly reveals this anger and expresses the way eyes can penetrate to the heart of a person, stripping away the masks and seeing the person as he or she is. Saying the feet are like burnished bronze is a metaphorical way of describing the immovable power of Christ.

Verse 19. The letter continues with the highest praise for the church. Christ says he knows their works; then he defines them as "love, faith, service, and patient endurance." Notice that love, faith, and patience are qualities of one's inner self. Service, then, flows out of these as a natural lifestyle. Ask: *In what ways are love, faith, service, and patient endurance characteristics of our church? of your life?*

The letter also includes Christ's congratulations for their spiritual growth that has resulted in greater works. "I know," says Christ, "that your last works are greater than the first." This statement forms an interesting contrast to what was said to the church at Ephesus, whose members were reprimanded for falling away (2:4-5).

Verse 20. The church at Thyatira has a problem, however: They are tolerating the woman Jezebel. There are many questions about this woman, but first let us see what we do know about her:

(1) She is a member of the church and has great influence among the membership.

(2) She calls herself a prophet, a word defined as "a spokesperson for God." In both the Old and the New Testaments, there are references to female prophets. Therefore, it would be no surprise to the congregation for a woman to announce she was a prophet. The problem arises, however, when people believe and follow her teachings thinking she is truly "a spokesperson for God."

(3) From the letter we glean that Jezebel did not want to destroy the church but wished to bring in new ideas and ways that, if implemented, would destroy the faith.

Now, what do we *not* know about Jezebel?

(1) We have no idea who she was, although we do have an idea about the kind of person she was.

(2) Another unanswered question relates to her name. Is *Jezebel* her real name, or is she a woman like Jezebel in the Old Testament? The Old Testament Jezebel was the daughter of Ethbaal, king of Sidon,

and the wife of Ahab, king of Israel. When she cam[e] from Sidon, she brought her native gods, Baal an[d] Astarte, with her and corrupted the faith of Israel wit[h] "whoredoms and sorceries" (2 Kings 9:22).

Jezebel killed the prophets of the Lord (1 King[s] 18:13) and fed at her table four hundred prophets o[f] Asherah (1 Kings 18:19). She meticulously planne[d] the murder of Naboth in order that Ahab might be i[n] possession of the ground where Naboth's vineyar[d] stood (1 Kings 21:1-16). It is hard to believe such ev[il] existed in one human being. Seeing her nature wil[l] help us understand the seriousness of the problem th[at] woman like Jezebel created in Thyatira.

Here Jezebel is accused of teaching two things—for[ni]cation and eating food that has been sacrificed t[o] idols. Why would there be a problem with eating foo[d] offered to an idol? Paul deals at length with this issu[e] in 1 Corinthians 8–10.

Paul told the Corinthian Christians that they "kno[w] 'no idol in the world really exists,' and that 'there is n[o] God but one' " (1 Corinthians 8:4); but not everyon[e] has this knowledge. Some people are so accustomed t[o] idols that they think "of the food they eat as foo[d] offered to an idol; and their conscience, being weak, i[s] defiled" (8:7). Paul suggests, "We are no worse off if w[e] do not eat, and no better off if we do" (8:8b). But her[e] is the important instruction: "Take care that this libert[y] of yours does not somehow become a stumbling bloc[k] to the weak" (8:9). Later he adds, "Therefore, if food i[s] a cause of their falling, I will never eat meat, so tha[t] I may not cause one of them to fall" (8:13). A Christia[n] has freedom, but this new lifestyle is centered in lov[e] that always seeks the highest good for others. S[o] a Christian does nothing that would cause another per[son] to misunderstand the Christian faith. Eating mea[t] that has been offered to idols may cause confusion as t[o] the nature of Christian faith and the belief in only on[e] God. Therefore, do not eat meat.

Another important issue arises here. Gentiles wer[e] in the church at Thyatira. In connection with them th[e] church had no doubt as to where a Christian's duty la[y]. Abstention from anything offered to idols was on[e] of the conditions required of Gentiles who wante[d] to join the Christian church (Acts 15:28-29).

In Thyatira this prohibition from eating mea[t] offered to idols placed the Christians in a precariou[s] situation. The Christian was cut off from most socia[l] fellowship with non-Christians. An idol worshipe[r] might invite friends over for a meal. A Christian migh[t] be one of those friends, but he or she could not eat th[e] sacrificed meat. This did not make Christians wante[d] uests. Or, on occasion, a worshiper would have a banquet for his friends in the pagan temple using the meat sacrificed to an idol. Here, again, a Christian could not participate.

In addition, there was another consequence of more serious proportions. Not eating meat offered to idols meant that a Christian could not join any trade guild, for all the guilds had a common meal as a central part of the organization. This meal might be held in a heathen temple precinct and consist principally of meat offered to idols. Yet, not to be a member of a trade guild was to commit economic suicide.

Here is where Jezebel and her teachings came in. She was saying that there was really no need for the Christians to cut themselves off this way, that they could be Christians and still belong to a trade union. They needed an income, the guild banquets, and fellowship with friends. Yet following such teaching meant forsaking the true God.

Ask: *Can you remember specific times when you have put personal interests before God's interest? If so, what was the situation? Are there times when the church has done this?*

The student book mentions that "in the Old Testament the words *fornication, prostitution,* and *adultery* are often employed to mean idolatry or apostasy" [page 26]. In Revelation 19:2, John specifically uses the word *fornication* to mean idolatry. In light of the situation in Thyatira, the word *fornication* appears to mean apostasy and idolatry here also. Therefore, Jezebel was apparently teaching that it was acceptable to participate in the emperor cult as well. Why not say, "Caesar is Lord" and burn a pinch of incense? You would not mean what you were saying. Just go through the ritual to fulfill the law.

Verse 21. In this verse we see how Christ yearns for Jezebel to teach truth, not lies. Christ says of Jezebel, "She refuses to repent of her fornication." She had an opportunity to return to true teaching. Instead, she continued urging on the church to a spiritual infidelity that would result in physical fornication. It was widely known that the common meals the trade guilds held were occasions for drunken revelry and loose morality. In addition, Jezebel telling people it was OK to participate in Caesar worship was encouraging spiritual bankruptcy. This woman was teaching doctrine that cannot be considered Christian.

Verses 22-23. The student book reminds us of the perplexing nature of these verses. Should we take them literally, or should we think of them as extended metaphors with messages beneath the words? It is important to know that the Book of Revelation is filled with metaphors that were familiar to the audience of the first century; it is you and I who must work hard in order to understand the language.

We see in these verses as well that evil has in itself the seeds of destruction. If Jezebel chooses to flaunt false teachings—eating meat offered to idols, participating in Caesar worship, being a part of the orgies of the trade guilds—there will be inevitable consequences for her and for those who follow her teachings.

The statement of Christ "I will strike her children dead" is a reference to the reality that people can be physically alive but spiritually dead. Those who are in "the deep things of Satan" (2:24) are dead to love, joy, kindness, peace, goodness, and other Christian patterns of life even though they are physically alive.

In verse 23b, Christ reveals again that he—not Jezebel, not Rome—is the one who searches minds and hearts and will give to each as he or she deserves. In Christian faith there is congruency of the mind, heart, and acts. In apostasy there are "works" that look good but come from an evil mind and heart. No doubt Jezebel seemed to many people to be a fine person. She called herself a prophet. She must have had a good presence and must have spoken well in order to exert such influence. The point is that Christ sees beyond the outward disguise.

Verse 24. The risen Christ tells the faithful that no additional burden will be laid on them. This statement implies that they carry a burden because of Jezebel and her influence. Any time there are conflicts in the church, all carry a burden.

Verses 25-28. These verses are a call for faithfulness until the day Christ comes. For those who do not succumb to temptation and who continue in Christian work, a twofold promise is given:

(1) "To everyone who conquers and continues to do my works to the end,

I will give authority over the nations;
    to rule them with an iron rod,
        as when clay pots are shattered"

is a reference from Psalm 2:8-9. It reflects the Jewish belief that the Messiah will conquer lands, smash the heathen, and extend the rule of Israel to the ends of the earth. Christ's promise is that through the Thyatirans' conquering (their faithfulness), he will make the nations their heritage.

(2) The second promise is the morning star. The symbolism behind this phrase is given in Revelation 22:16. There the Lord describes himself as "the bright morning star." The promise of the morning star is

Christ covenanting to give himself, which is the ultimate reward of Christians.

Verse 29. This verse contains the call for people to listen at the deepest level of hearing to what the Spirit is saying to the church. Doing so can make the difference between life and death.[1]

INTRODUCE OUR NEED

■ If the Christian church as a whole had accepted the teachings of Jezebel, Christianity would inevitably have become another of the religions of which the Roman Empire was so full; and the church would not exist today. As I travel to cities where these religions were once so powerful—Ephesus, Thessalonica, Corinth, Rome—the ruins of the magnificent temples and the broken and scattered pieces of the statues of the gods who were once worshiped in awe and reverence lie as a testimony to their former size and power. I give thanks to God for John, Paul, and others who had the courage to be God's messengers in a world that tried to silence THE MESSAGE but could not.

Where are the current results of the worship of Zeus, Diana, and the Roman emperor? These religions perished because they were the vision of human beings only.

Ask: *What are some teachings or positions of compromise that are prevalent among some people today that you consider to be inconsistent with Christian teachings?* (*The student book mentions several: gambling on football pools, enjoying the sexual self-gratification of the "entertainment" environment, practicing discrimination against people of other races, taking pride in status and wealth, engaging in shady business practices, loving material possessions, ignoring the needs of the unfortunate, and so forth. If you have brought newspaper clippings or magazine articles about false teachings, share them at this point.*)

LESSON PLAN

■ The student book tells us that the New Testament speaks of sound teaching as a mandate for Christian living and that teaching does not mean just doctrine but other areas of living. The lesson discusses in an insightful way five of these areas. I would like to add a sixth.

Christian living involves an openness to what the Spirit says to us. A closed mind and heart are dangerous. They leave us in chosen ignorance; rob us of mental, spiritual, and relational growth; take from others the gifts God wants to give through us; and breed self-

righteousness. The parable of the Pharisee and the tax collector (Luke 18:9-14) illustrates this point.

The tax collector is a despised man; the Pharisee is a respected member of the community, one who was considered very religious because he kept the outward laws. Look at the contrast between the two men as they go to the Temple to pray. The religious man (the Pharisee) prays, "God, I thank you that I am not like other people: thieves, rogues, adulterers, or even like this tax collector. I fast twice a week; I give a tenth of all my income" (18:11-12). The prayer stops here. Ask: *Is this a prayer? Why or why not?* (*In this prayer the Pharisee is simply announcing the "good" works that he has done. Maybe he is praying this prayer for the benefit of God; but, on the other hand, he may be praying so that the people in the Temple will hear him and think well of him. True prayer is "coming home" to God who has invited all persons into fellowship with him.*)

Look next at the prayer of the tax collector: "God be merciful to me, a sinner!" (18:13). The tax collector is open for new life. We can feel in him a "coming home" to God in simple honesty and great trust. He knows he is a sinner and openly confesses it with the hope and expectation of forgiveness. Indeed, he is not disappointed.

The Pharisee prayed with himself; the tax collector prayed with God. The Pharisee extolled his good works; the tax collector repented of his lifestyle. The Pharisee was blind to the work of God going on in his presence; the tax collector experienced the forgiveness of God.

The Pharisee is an example of what can happen when the mind and heart are closed to the fresh wind of the Spirit. Our lives become fertile soil for the growing of arrogance, prejudice, pride, self-righteousness, and a judgmental nature. Ask: *What similarities do you see between the Pharisee and Jezebel?* (*Both were members of an established religion, both were in positions of leadership, both were centered in self-promotion, spiritual infidelity was in both, concern for the well-being of the religious community and the individuals who comprise it was not in evidence.*)

Another result of living with a mind and soul closed to the fresh wind of the Spirit is stagnation and solidification of our theology (our concept of God). Content with what we have, we choose to stay there and not entertain any deeper knowledge. When new ideas are presented, they are immediately dismissed with names like liberal, conservative, atheistic, of the devil, and so forth. We find satisfaction in the comfort zone and see no reason to move out of it. To think in this way is to choose to live in the flatlands when we are called to scale the Himalayas of the spirit. What we do and who we are is ultimately determined by what we think and by what we hold to be of supreme value.

Sound Christian teaching embodied in daily living and worship is essential in the faith. "Jezebel-living"—convincing people that they could live like pagans and still call themselves Christians—cannot be tolerated. Anyone who attempts to promote such practices should be silenced.

Ask: *What are some practices and theological teachings that you consider out of line with Christian teaching?* (*I attended the funeral of a five-year-old girl who drowned in a pond near where she lived. When the pastor stood up to deliver the message, he called the parents by name and said, "God drowned your child in order to bring you to him." I wanted to shout for all to hear, "God did not do such a thing. God is weeping over the loss of the child and seeks to comfort the parents." The class members will have other experiences to share.*)

Another important question needs to be discussed in order to touch the everydayness of life. How does one know when teaching is sound? All committed Christians ask this question because there are many facets to consider in every decision.

When Paul was faced with a variety of teachings that were not sound, he gave some key questions for people to ask themselves (1 Corinthians 10:23–11:1):

(1) Is this beneficial?
(2) Does this build up?
(3) Is this to the advantage of others?
(4) Does it offend the conscience of another person?
(5) Does it bring glory to God?
(6) Does this imitate the life and teaching of Jesus Christ?

These questions are not simple. They require thought, knowledge of others, care for the well-being of people, a willingness to sacrifice, and a centering in Christ.

Another avenue of discerning if teaching is sound is prayer. We are created with the ability to know God and to have communion with God. God invites us into this relationship. Through this relationship people can count on the guidance of God for discernment. When there is openness like this, we know when the answer is God's will because there is peace within.

To close the session, lead the class members in singing "I Want a Principle Within." Then pray the prayer at the end of the lesson in the student book.

---

[1] Information in "Bible Background" drawn from *The Revelation of John*, Volume 1, by William Barclay (The Westminster Press, 1976); pages 101–11.

TRY ANOTHER METHOD

■ Instead of reading the parable of the Pharisee and the tax collector (Luke 18:9-14), have it presented in the form of a roleplay. As you know, drama is a powerful medium for the message.

Chapter Four

GOOD NEWS, BAD NEWS

PURPOSE

To affirm that the gospel offers words of comfort and encouragement and words of reproof and discipline

BIBLE PASSAGE

Revelation 3:7-10, 15-21
Background: Revelation 3:7-22

CORE VERSE
I know your works. (Revelation 3:8, 15)

GET READY

■ Have a map of Asia Minor on hand so you can point out the locations of Philadelphia and Laodicea.

List on a chalkboard or on a large piece of paper the names of the seven churches to whom Revelation was written. Also list the problem discussed in each church's letter (see below). Can you locate a common thread in the list? Could it be lack of commitment and faithfulness to Christ?

The Seven Churches and Their Problems

Ephesus:	danger of losing the love they had at first
Smyrna:	fear of suffering
Pergamum:	doctrinal compromise
Thyatira:	moral issues
Sardis:	spiritual deadness
Philadelphia:	failure to hold fast
Laodicea:	lukewarmness

BIBLE BACKGROUND

■ The history of the ancient city of Philadelphia is interesting indeed. Knowing this rich background opens up the meaning of many words and phrases in the letter to the church at Philadelphia. Philadelphia was the youngest of the seven cities to whom Revelation was originally written. It was founded in the second century B.C. by Eumenes II, ruler of Pergamum, or perhaps by his brother Attalus II whose loyalty had earned him the name *Philadelphos,* which means "one who loves his brother." The city of Philadelphia was named for him.

Philadelphia was located on the edge of a great plain whose soil was quite fertile. Philadelphia was the center of a prolific grape-growing area and a producer of delectable wines. However, in A.D. 17, there came a great earthquake that destroyed Sardis, as well as ten other cities, and almost completely devastated Philadelphia. Tremors were experienced for years afterward. Frightened by the constant tremors, many people moved out of the city to areas that were considered to be safer. By the time Revelation was written, Philadelphia had been rebuilt; and within the city there was a Christian congregation.

Revelation 3:7. The letter to the church at Philadelphia is addressed the same way the other letters are—"to the angel of the church." The pastor or another leader is the recipient. The writing begins with three titles for the one whose words are in the letter, the risen Christ:

(1) "The Holy One"
(2) "The True One"
(3) The one "who has the key of David, who opens and no one will shut, who shuts and no one opens"

The *Holy One* is used many times in the Old Testament as a name for God.

> Holy, holy, holy is the LORD of hosts.
> (Isaiah 6:3)

> To whom then will you compare me,
> or who is my equal? says the Holy One.
> (Isaiah 40:25)

> I am the LORD, your Holy One,
> the Creator of Israel, your King.
> (Isaiah 43:15)

The word *holy* means set apart, separate, different, unique. God is holy because God has a quality of being that is uniquely God's. A study of world religions verifies this truth. There were gods who demanded human sacrifice, gods whose worshipers practiced sexual orgies, gods who preyed on the fears and superstitions of people. In no way could these gods be called holy.

In the Old Testament the words *Holy One* refer to God who is unique, different, and set apart from all others. And, as Revelation states, God's Son is also the Holy One; for Jesus reveals the nature of God.

The second title, the *True One*, comes from a Greek word that means real as opposed to that which is unreal. In Jesus Christ we have reality, the "True One" from God and the "True One" who is the nature of God.

In the third title "the key" is a symbol of authority and power. To hold a key is to have the power to lock or to unlock, to open or to close doors. The image given here comes from Isaiah 22:22. King Hezekiah had a faithful steward named Eliakim who alone could allow persons access to the king. Isaiah heard God say of Eliakim, "I will place on his shoulder the key of the house of David; he shall open, and no one shall shut; he shall shut, and no one shall open" (Isaiah 22:22). By using this reference, Revelation is saying that Christ is God's faithful steward, the one who opens the door for people to have access to God and who holds the key to the city of David, the New Jerusalem.[1]

Verse 8. The church at Philadelphia was poor, small, and besieged with problems; but its members had been faithful. Christ was aware of this: "I know your works." Then follows a great declaration: "I have set before you an open door." In the Christian context the open door signifies the door of missionary opportunity (1 Corinthians 16:8-9; 2 Corinthians 2:12; Colossians 4:3).

In addition, there is good reason to believe the "open door" is a reference to the purpose of the founding of the city of Philadelphia. It was specifically established for the purpose of spreading the Greek language and culture to Lydia and Phrygia, which it did quite well. To accomplish this mission, Philadelphia was located where the borders of Phrygia, Lydia, and Mysia met (which gave the church at Philadelphia an open door for her missionary enterprise as well). Use a map to identify the location.

The risen Christ calls the citizens of Philadelphia to a second missionary enterprise: "Look, I have set before you an open door, which no one is able to shut" (Revelation 3:8b)—an open door to spread to people beyond the borders of Philadelphia the love of God and the good news of salvation through Christ.

Verse 9. The missionary enterprise of the church, however, had met with opposition from some Jews who rejected the Christians' beliefs. Christ says these are not true Jews, and they are being condemned for their attitude toward and their treatment of the Christians. The day will come when these Jews will bow down to the church. At that time they will learn that the church is loved by "the true one," Christ.

Verse 10. A reward is promised to this little church for their faithfulness. The reward will be manifest in the "hour of trial that is coming." Christ will keep them in this time. This is not a promise that special protection will be given but that the risen Christ will be with them in the time of trouble. Ask: *Can you identify a time of trial when you experienced being kept in the loving care of Christ? If so, what were the circumstances?*

We now turn to Laodicea, the seventh and last church on the list. Laodicea was about forty miles southeast of Philadelphia. It was founded by Antiochus II of Syria in the third century B.C. and was named for his wife, Laodice. This city had several unique characteristics that definitely left their mark on the letter to the church.

(1) Laodicea was a rich commercial center noted especially for its clothing manufacture. The sheep around the city were famous for their raven-black wool. This wool was used to mass produce outer garments.

(2) The city was the chief medical center of Phrygia, having doctors with reputations that drew people from a wide area to Laodicea. The medical center was also famous for two medicines—salve for the eyes and ointment for the ears. Exporting these two products was big business for the Laodiceans.

(3) The city was a banking and financial center of great importance, making it one of the wealthiest cities in the world.

The church at Laodicea has the distinction of being the only church about which the risen Christ has nothing good to say. There is no redeeming feature identified in the church.

Verses 15-16. Have you ever lifted a glass of water to your mouth expecting to drink a cool, refreshing liquid only to find that the water is lukewarm? Immediately, you want to spit it out. You feel great disappointment. This is the way the risen Christ feels about the church at Laodicea. There is indifference in the congregation. The people are not committed to the teachings of Jesus, and they are not opposed to them. Christ urges them to be one way or the other, indicating that not to be on the journey of faith is preferable to the way they are living.

Verse 17. The faith center of the church in Laodicea was wealth and prosperity; the people were comfortable and completely self-satisfied. However, the risen Christ declares them to be in spiritual poverty; they are "wretched, pitiable, poor, blind, and naked." In the midst of wealth that came from making clothes, these people had become naked; in the midst of prosperity that came from exporting eye salve, they had become blind; in the midst of financial wealth, the Laodiceans had become poor.

Verse 18. Christ admonishes the church to refocus its center of faith in three ways:

(1) Gold refined by fire is to be bought from him. "Buying" here is used in the figurative sense, for the gold Christ gives cannot be bought with money. It is the "gold" (riches) of faith that comes from the refiner's fire of faithfulness.

(2) White robes are to be bought to cover their nakedness. This is an interesting statement; in the ancient world, to be stripped naked was the worst of humiliations. "Buying" again is in the figurative sense because the white robe is a reference to the beauty and purity of the inner life. Beautiful outer garments cannot beautify that person whose inward nature is indifferent to love, joy, concern for others, and faithfulness.

(3) The third admonition is to buy salve to anoint eyes that are now blind so that sight is restored. The church is blinded to the mission and ministry of Christ in the world. This is a deadly condition; unless their blindness is cured, they will cease to exist.

Verse 19. An abrupt change in speaking occurs; there is tenderness in these words. The risen Christ equates discipline with love. This verse could be paraphrased, "It is those who are dearest to me on whom I will exercise the greatest discipline." Then Christ encourages the Laodiceans to repent and return to the

One who continually seeks a meaningful relationship with them.

Verse 20. This verse opens with an exclamation—"Listen!"—another way of telling the Laodiceans to pay close attention; for something important is coming. Indeed this is true; Christ tells them he is standing at the door of their hearts knocking, waiting for them to open the door and to allow him to enter. When Christ is allowed in, they will eat together. What a meaningful image this evoked in the minds of those who first heard the letter. In the Middle East, to eat with someone means you are friends for life. Christ is asking to have a lifetime relationship with the congregation at Laodicea. Ask: *In what ways do our times of eating together at church reflect the Middle Eastern tradition of being friends for life?*

Verse 21. The promise of the risen Christ is that the one who is victorious will sit with him on the throne. In the ancient Near East, a throne was more like a couch than it was like a chair. Isn't this a beautiful image, sharing fellowship with Christ for eternity?

INTRODUCE OUR NEED

■ Charlotte, North Carolina, and the surrounding area were greatly excited when Mother Teresa of Calcutta, India, came to speak. This frail octogenarian made the list of the world's most-admired women on many occasions, but she would have been the first to say such an honor should not come to her. The deepest desire of her heart was to be God's servant. When someone asked Mother Teresa about retirement, her response was, "I am a pencil in the hand of God. God does the writing." You see in her an example of a person who was totally surrendered to God. To be in her presence was to experience the love and grace of God. In Charlotte more people came to hear Mother Teresa speak than attend most of the sporting events held there. To me this fact illustrates the yearning of people to hear persons of integrity and character share their faith.

On one of Mother Teresa's visits to America, she told about her work among the poor and dying of India. After the service several people volunteered to go to India and to be a part of the ministry there. She deeply appreciated their selfless offers but said, "I would like for you to go to India with me, but you are needed much more in America. You see, you have a poverty here that we do not know; it is the poverty of affluence."

"The poverty of affluence" is a haunting phrase

because it is true. How like the church at Laodicea we are. Our affluence has made spiritual paupers of us. Ask the questions on page 35 in the student book: *"What are some of the signs of lethargy in your church? in yourself? Can anything be done? If so, what?"*

LESSON PLAN

■ As you studied the Bible passage, did you feel you were looking at churches in your area? As problems were identified, did you say, "I know a church like that" or "That is my problem"? The material in our Bible passage is the "stuff" that concerns churches. Yet the lesson is not one of despair but of hope, for the bad news can become good news through Christ. (Use the optional method about writing a letter to your church here if you have planned in advance.)

Discuss the story in the student book about the writer's father spanking him when he shot an arrow at his father's legs [pages 31–32]. Ask: *How is God like that father?* (*God is patient. God tries many ways to encourage obedience. God loves us so much that punishment is given for our own good.*)

Do you know the song "Love Is a Many Splendored Thing"? It talks about the magnificence of love and how all of life is enhanced through loving relationships. Our Bible passage incorporates such a concept. The truth is that about the time we think we have an understanding of the love of God, another dimension is revealed; and we realize that God's love is unending, undefinable, and inexhaustible.

In the comic strips of the daily newspaper, there used to be a one-frame picture with the caption "Love Is . . ." Each day there was a different description of the word: Love is a puppy. Love is a handshake. Love is a letter. Figurines carried on this idea. Each figurine depicted a child giving an expression of love. I received one of these figurines as a gift, and it speaks quite clearly in expressing one facet of love. My figurine is of a little child sitting on a bench reading a book, which she holds with one hand. In the other hand she holds an ice cream cone. Sitting next to the child is a puppy who is licking the ice cream cone. The caption says, "Love Is Sharing."

Let us now experience how the seven letters of the Book of Revelation complete the phrase "Love is . . ."

Love is knowledge. In speaking to each of the seven churches, the risen Christ says, "I know":

—*To Ephesus:* "I know your works, your toil and your patient endurance. I know that you cannot tolerate evildoers" (2:2).

—*To Smyrna:* "I know your affliction and your poverty, even though you are rich" (2:9).

—*To Pergamum:* "I know where you are living, where Satan's throne is" (2:13).

—*To Thyatira:* "I know your works—your love, faith, service, and patient endurance. I know that your last works are greater than the first" (2:19).

—*To Sardis:* "I know your works; you have a name of being alive, but you are dead" (3:1).

—*To Philadelphia:* "I know your works. Look, I have set before you an open door, which no one is able to shut" (3:8).

—*To Laodicea:* "I know your works; you are neither cold nor hot. I wish that you were either cold or hot" (3:15).

What fantastic insight is given through these words! They teach us that Christ enters the arena in which each of us lives and knows us in our goodness and in our badness. We do not have to become good enough before Christ comes to us; the risen Christ meets us where we are. Through this relationship Christ knows us as we are and is able to advise, encourage, admonish, and discipline.

In life and in death God knows us and is with us. We are never alone. The question then becomes, Am I open to receive God who stands at the door and knocks, wanting to be invited in? Ask: *What experiences have you had of becoming aware of God knowing you and the arena in which you live?*

Love is forgiveness. The letters to the seven churches reveal that several of these churches were not what a church should be. Within them were problems of false teaching, indifference, tolerance of wrong doctrines, love of money and possessions, and so forth. Yet the student book reminds us that even though they had failed, Christ had not abandoned them. In these situations Christ calls the church to repentance:

—*Ephesus:* "Remember then from what you have fallen; repent, and do the works you did at first" (2:5).

—*Sardis:* "Remember then what you received and heard; obey it, and repent" (3:3).

—*Laodicea:* "I reprove and discipline those whom I love. Be earnest, therefore, and repent" (3:19).

Isn't it wonderful to know that the backslider, be it an individual or a church, is welcome to rejoin the family as a full member with all the benefits restored.

A pastor friend called me recently to tell about a letter he received from a man in prison. The prisoner wrote that he soon would be released and inquired if there was room in the church for an ex-con and his family. The pastor said he wrote immediately, "I have just taken a poll of the congregation, and they say there is room for another sinner saved by grace."

Love is forgiveness; therefore, "Christ does not consign those to eternal punishment who will show any inclination to seek restoration. He loves not only the faithful but also those who have fallen away" [student book; page 36].

Love is an "open door." The risen Christ revealed to the church at Philadelphia that he had set before them an open door. God gives open doors because God loves all people and yearns for a relationship with each one. God would be cruel if his love went to only a few. The overall plan of God is to give "open doors" through which people go to share the "good news" and thereby overcome "bad news."

Often, we think of this open door as being a call to some distant country. It may be that, but the call to the members of the church at Philadelphia was to move through the open door where they were. The mission field is in our home, among our friends, on the job, at the supermarket, in our recreation. Anywhere people are, there is God's call to walk through the open door to missionary service. Ask: *In what ways is this being done in our church? in our class? by you as an individual?*

Love is prayer. In the act of Creation humans were uniquely made. Genesis tells us that God said, "Let us make humankind in our image" (Genesis 1:26). The Creator did not abandon the creation but sought and seeks to establish a meaningful relationship with those created. God is love, and such love invites people into fellowship. One of the channels for this to happen is prayer.

The challenge issued to the churches—to repent, to discern, to move through the open door, to be faithful—cannot be accomplished through human power; divine energy is required. Prayer is the way we communicate with God in order to be given this ability. Prayer is coming home to the One who created us in order that we may leave home with the tools and the power for the task.

Richard Foster told an interesting story that illustrates this point. A man was in a shopping mall with his two-year-old son. The child was particularly fussy that day. The frustrated father tried to calm the child but to no avail. Finally, he picked up his son, held him close to his chest, and began singing to him. The words did not rhyme, and the tune had no melody; but the father was sharing his heart. "I love you," he sang. "I'm so glad you are my boy. You make me happy. I like the way you laugh." The father continued to sing as they went from store to store. The child eventually relaxed and became still. When shopping was finished, they went to the car. As the father prepared to buckle his son into the car seat, the child lifted his head and said, "Sing it to me again, Daddy! Sing it again."[2]

This is what prayer is—allowing ourselves to be gathered into the arms of God and to listen to God's love song for us. It may sound off key and the words may not rhyme, but that does not matter; we are home. Ask: *What does it mean to say, "We are home"? When do we feel most at home?* (*To be at home is to feel fully accepted and understood as we are. We feel most at home when the resources of home are given and we, in total openness, receive.*)

To close the session, sing "Love Divine, All Loves Excelling." Then pray the prayer at the end of the lesson in the student book.

---

[1] Information above drawn from *The Revelation of John*, Volume 1, by William Barclay (The Westminster Press, 1976); pages 125–28.
[2] From *Prayer*, by Richard Foster (Harper San Francisco, 1992); page 3.

TRY ANOTHER METHOD

■ An effective way to present the issues of the churches at Philadelphia and Laodicea would be to ask two members of the class to read the letters aloud, one at a time. Ask the class to be the congregation of that church. When each letter is read, ask the congregation to respond.

Early in the week ask each member of the class to consider what he or she thinks Christ would say in a letter to the church you attend. During the session, invite members to contribute ideas to a joint letter. If they are willing, share the letter with the pastor and other church members.

Chapter Five

WHO IS WORTHY?

PURPOSE

To help us more deeply appreciate the sacrificial life and death of Jesus Christ

BIBLE PASSAGE

Revelation 5:1-10
Background: Revelation 4–5

CORE VERSE

By your blood you ransomed for God
    saints from every tribe and
    language and people and nation.
                        (Revelation 5:9)

GET READY

■ If possible, the worship center might have a variety of pictures of Jesus arranged in a way that each class member can see them. Choose the traditional pictures but also some that are not so familiar.

Try to locate a picture of a papyrus scroll to illustrate the scroll in the Bible passage. Someone who has traveled to Egypt may have purchased a piece of papyrus. If so, ask him or her to bring it to the session.

Write Revelation 5:9-10 on a chalkboard or on a large piece of paper for the class members to focus on when you are discussing the "New Song."

BIBLE BACKGROUND

■ We move now from Chapters 2 and 3 in the Book of Revelation in which the risen Christ addresses the churches on earth to Chapters 4 and 5, which take place in the court of heaven. The symbols up to now have been relatively easy to understand, but now we move into more difficult and complex imagery. The student book reminds us that the early church may have found it much easier to understand this imagery than we do because the Book of Revelation "was written about circumstances in which they lived and in a symbolic language with which they were familiar" [page 41].

Chapter 4 opens with a vision of a service of heavenly worship in praise of God, the Almighty. In Chapter 5, the vision continues and is in praise of Jesus, the Lamb, who is given the highest honor in heaven and on earth—the breaking of the seven seals on the scroll.

Revelation 5:1. In the account of John's vision, the focus is first on the right hand of God, which holds a scroll with writing on the front and on the back. The scroll is sealed with seven seals. This vision is taken from Ezekiel 2:9-10: "I looked, and a hand was stretched out to me, and a written scroll was in it. He spread it before me; it had writing on the front and on the back, and written on it were words of lamentation and mourning and woe."

In the ancient world, and down to the second century A.D., writing was done on papyrus, a paperlike substance made from the pith of a bulrush that grew in the area of the Nile. Papyrus was very expensive; so if a person had a great deal to write, he or she wrote on the front and on the back. When a scroll was finished, it was fastened with threads and the threads were sealed at the knots.

A scroll with seven seals, as in John's vision, was

a will. Roman law required seven witnesses to seal the scroll, each with the witness's own seal. The scroll could be opened only when all seven witnesses or their designated legal representatives were present. According to this custom the scroll in the hand of God would be God's written will for the affairs of the universe. The student book mentions that seven seals are spoken of in other apocalyptic literature and used as a means "to warn people about coming woes and disasters" [page 42].

The seals could have another meaning as well. Since "seven" means perfect or complete in apocalyptic writing, it is possible that the seven seals are used to illustrate the point that the scroll's contents are completely hidden from everyone so that "no one in heaven or on earth or under the earth was able to open the scroll or to look into it" (Revelation 5:3).

Verses 2-3. As John was looking at the scroll, a "mighty" messenger of God, an angel with a loud voice, appeared asking the question, "Who is worthy to open the scroll and break its seals?" The angel would have to be strong and his voice would have to have great volume because the question was not just for heaven but for earth and under the earth, the entire universe. In response to the challenge of the angel, no one came forth; no one felt adequate or worthy to break the seals on God's scroll.

Verse 4. Upon seeing this, John tells us that he began to weep bitterly because such a person did not come forth. There are two possible reasons for John's bitter crying:

(1) In Revelation 4:1b, a promise was given to John: "Come up here, and I will show you what must take place after this." It now looked like this plan might be thwarted.

(2) John is mightily concerned that the whole universe is so evil, so far from God's plan for humankind, that there is no one to whom God can give the written will.

Verse 5. While John was weeping, one of the elders came to him and said, "Do not weep." (For background on the twenty-four elders who surrounded the throne of God, refer to page 41 of the student book.) He tells John that there is one who is able to open the scroll and the seven seals—Jesus Christ. This is possible because Jesus has won the victory over death and evil through his complete obedience to God. Such obedience has bestowed on him two titles—"the Lion of the tribe of Judah, the Root of David."

"The Lion of Judah" has roots that go back to Jacob's final blessing of his sons before his death. In

the blessing of Judah, Jacob says, "Judah is a lion's whelp" (Genesis 49:9). Down through the years the Jews began to use "the Lion of Judah" as a messianic title for the one who would come and usher in the messianic age. In using this title for Jesus, the elder is saying, "This is he, the Messiah. This is why he can open the scroll and its seven seals."

Jesus is also called "the Root of David." This title also has Old Testament origins. In Isaiah 11:1-2, there is the prophecy,

A shoot shall come out from the stump of Jesse,
    and a branch shall grow out of his roots.
The spirit of the Lord shall rest on him,
    the spirit of wisdom and understanding,
    the spirit of counsel and might,
    the spirit of knowledge and the fear of the
        Lord.

Jesse was the father of David, and the Jews expected the Messiah to come from his lineage. Therefore, "the Root of David" was also a title for the Messiah. The elder uses two titles that are uniquely Jewish to identify Jesus as the Messiah, the one who can preside over the working out of the contents of the scroll of God. Ask: *What are some titles that you would give to Jesus?*

Verse 6. What follows is totally unexpected, even unthinkable. John expects to see the Lion of Judah, but instead he sees a Lamb. He expects to see power and force; instead he sees sacrifice and slaughter. The Jews expected a Messiah who would break the yoke of Roman tyranny and liberate them, but there is nothing of this in the vision.

What does this vision say about the messianic age? Instead of coming with power and force that kills, destroys, and inflicts pain on innocent people, he, the Messiah, is a sacrificial lamb; he will take on himself the hurts of humankind and will rule with sacrificial love.

Jesus lived out this concept when he rode into Jerusalem on a donkey on Palm Sunday. Kings who came to battle rode horses and carried weapons. Persons who came in peace rode a donkey. Ask: *Do we still have difficulty with this concept? Do we still think of power, weapons, and aggression as the way to solve our problems? Why or why not?*

In the vision Jesus is seen as a Lamb. The Lamb has seven horns that stand for perfect omnipotence, perfect power, and perfect honor. The Lamb also has seven eyes, and the eyes are the spirits of God dispatched into all the earth. This is the apocalyptic way of saying that there is no place in the universe that is not under the eye of God. It shows the omniscience of God.

Verse 7. The Lamb now takes the scroll from the right hand of God, and its contents will be revealed for all to know.

Verse 8. At this time the four living creatures and the twenty-four elders bow in honor of the Lamb. The four creatures represent all that is in nature; the elders represent the universal church. Each of the elders holds a harp and golden bowls of incense. The harp was the traditional instrument used for singing psalms. "Praise the LORD with the lyre; / make melody to him with the harp of ten strings," says the psalmist (Psalm 33:2). The golden bowls full of incense are the prayers of God's faithful people on earth. The likening of prayers to incense is a tradition of the Jews. Incense was frequently used as people prayed so that the prayers would be pleasing to the nostrils of God. The Psalms mention prayers as incense, for example,

> Let my prayer be counted as incense before you,
> and the lifting up of my hands as an evening
> sacrifice.
>
> (Psalm 141:2)

Participation in worship on earth is connected with worship in heaven. The prayers of the believer on earth are mixed with those of all the hosts of heaven.

Ask: *What does this vision say to you about prayer?* (*It speaks of the importance of prayer. Our prayers are a part of a universal prayer chain. Our prayers are given to Christ. Our prayers on earth are a part of the prayers of heaven.*)

Verses 9-10. The song that the creatures and elders sing is a new song. One of the characteristics of the Book of Revelation is the emphasis on new things—the new name, the New Jerusalem, the new heaven, and the new earth. We also find the promise that God will make all things new, and there are new songs.

The song begins with the creatures and elders praising the death of Jesus for the following reasons:

(1) Jesus' death was a sacrificial death with a purpose. Through the giving up of his life, the broken relationship between God and humankind was restored.

(2) Jesus' death was an emancipating death. According to the New Testament, it cost the death of Jesus to rescue humankind from the slavery and degradation caused by sin.

(3) The death of Jesus was universal in scope. It was not just for the Jews but for every race and nationality on the globe. The creatures and elders sing praise that "saints from every tribe and language and people and nation" can be ransomed (Revelation 5:9). Indeed, this is a new song!

The New Song continues with the giving of new titles to ransomed people—priests and citizens of the kingdom of God. The first-century church was composed mostly of the poor and the outcasts of society, people who had little hope of attaining significance in the world. The New Song brings new identity, even new citizenship; for they are citizens in the kingdom of God. In the ancient world priests alone had access to God. Ordinary Jews could go no farther in the Temple than the Court of the Israelites; they were denied entrance into the Court of the Priests. The New Song affirms the priesthood of all believers.

It is easy to believe the vision is speaking of the future alone, not of the present. Yet this is not the case; for the song says,

> You have made them to be a kingdom and priests
> serving our God,
> and they will reign on earth.
>
> (Revelation 5:10)

The Book of Revelation is not speaking of victorious living as the world conceives it—political victory, material possessions, high-salaried positions. It is speaking of a kingdom of love, joy, meaningfulness, special relationships, selfless living, and hope that the risen Christ brought through his sacrificial death. It is victorious living in the midst of any circumstances.

When we think of what the death and resurrection of Jesus has done and is doing for the whole world, it is no wonder that the creatures and elders burst into song.[1]

INTRODUCE OUR NEED

■ I was returning from teaching Bible at the Wyoming Annual Conference. Seated next to me on the plane was a young man wearing a military uniform. When I asked if he was a Marine, he replied, "Yes." Then he told me he was on his way back to his base to be mustered out of the Marines due to some new regulations. He said he was devastated because all he had ever wanted was to be a career Marine. Now he did not know what the future held for him; he did not know where to go or what to do.

I asked if he knew anything about Jesus, to which he

replied, "No." What a privilege it was to share with him the good news about One who had been seeking a relationship with him all his life—One who does not make our world end up "and you live happily ever after" (that is only in story books) but One who is a friend, a guide, a savior.

As we talked, I realized this young man had not been in Sunday school or church; and all his contacts with Christianity had been negative. As he heard about Jesus, his interest was intense and expectant. It was wonderful to watch his response to the idea that someone loved him as he was and wanted a personal relationship with him.

When we arrived at the airport where I got off, our conversation was not finished. I asked if he would mind if a pastor came to see him to finish the story. He said he would like that. When I got to my office, I called a pastor who serves close to Camp LeJeune and asked if he would go that evening and talk with this young man. He did; and in the days that followed, the young man decided to become a Christian. Now he has a relationship with Christ that makes every day a time of meaning and joy regardless of the external circumstances.

As I reflect on this event, I realize that we all live on the mission field. Many people in America have not heard the good news we are studying: Christ is the one who is worthy to open the will of God and to reveal its contents. Ask: *How are we trying to get this message of hope to people who do not attend church?*

LESSON PLAN

■ The Book of Revelation gives rich and varied pictures of Christ. We see that he is the fulfillment of the hopes and dreams of the Jewish community, for he is the Lion of Judah and the Root of David. He is the one who is worthy to take the scroll of God, to break the seals, and to reveal God's plan for the universe. Jesus is the Lamb who is all powerful and all seeing but willing to be crucified in order to reconcile humankind to God. Jesus is the worthy one!

How do you put into a picture or into language a description of the One who possesses all these characteristics? Paul tried when he wrote, "He is the image of the invisible God, the firstborn of all creation; for in him all things in heaven and on earth were created" (Colossians 1:15-16). In another passage we read, "For in him all the fullness of God was pleased to dwell" (Colossians 1:19). Ask: *How would you speak of Jesus Christ? How would you define him and his mission?*

We speak about culture shock, which can be defined as new norms in culture that negate previous norms. For example, my husband was taught to remove his hat when entering a house or when eating. Young people think nothing of wearing a hat in the home or at the table. This is culture shock for Bill. Jesus certainly produced culture shock among both Jews and Gentiles; for he brought new definitions to old clearly defined words, customs, and concepts. Let's examine some of them.

For centuries the Jews believed and taught that they were God's chosen people. They believed there would be a day when their Messiah would usher in the messianic age by crushing their captors with might and weapons and thus set them free. This day was anticipated with joy and high expectations for rewards.

However, Jesus taught that the messianic kingdom was the activity of God released in the world *now* and in the *future*. He taught that the Kingdom is characterized by love, peace, forgiveness, joy, caring relationships, being a neighbor. The Messiah will not be one who crushes the enemy with might. The Messiah's self-giving love will go out to all persons, not just to one select group. Is it any wonder, then, that in the Book of Acts we find a report of the Thessalonians dragging Christians before the city authorities and shouting, "These people who have been turning the world upside down have come here also" (Acts 17:6)?

The Jews taught that worship included the sacrifice of animals. Jesus taught that true worship results in the sacrifice of the self.

Only persons of a certain rank and status could enter the Court of the Priests. Jesus taught that all persons have access to God.

The Jews taught that they would one day judge, punish, and control the earth. We believe that all things in heaven and on earth were created through Christ and for Christ. All the earth was made to operate according to the life and teachings of Jesus.

A sheepherder in Utah wrote the following letter to a radio station:

Dear Program Director:
I am out in the fields and hills all day long with my sheep. All I have with me is my battery-powered radio and my old violin. I listen to your station and enjoy it very much. I need to ask a favor of you. You see, my violin is out of tune; and I have nothing to tune it by. One day would you interrupt your program and play A 440 so that I can get my violin back in tune?

Imagine how happy the sheepherder must have

been when he heard this announcement on the radio: "For the sheepherder out in Utah; in five minutes we will play A 440 so you can tune your violin."

Jesus is God's A 440 to the world. Humankind was so out of tune that it needed the international tuning note so that people could become members of God's great orchestra. Ask: *What are indications of a life being out of tune?* (*The class members may mention feeling that life has no meaning, being judgmental, abusing drugs, being violent, feeling sad and hopeless, having low self-esteem, abusing power, and being self-centered.*)

How do we get back in tune? John Wesley, the founder of Methodism, would certainly have enjoyed answering this question, for at the center of his life was a deep concern for the lost. Wesley believed God called all people to be in right relationship with him. Therefore, the task of the church was to preach the good news to the lost. Perhaps a way to answer the question, How do we get in tune? would be to look at John Wesley's doctrine of atonement.

Wesley believed that humankind was created in the image of God; therefore people were good. But this state did not continue. Because of the misuse of free will (sin), the state of goodness was lost. This meant that the original state of nature no longer existed. For Wesley sin was basic and pervaded all humankind. Sinfulness is a condition that one cannot conquer alone; one must accept the work of Jesus Christ.

Because God's nature is love, the beginning work of salvation is God's prevenient grace. The word *prevenient* means "to come before." God comes to us first, seeking a relationship. Prevenient grace seeks a response, but humankind has the free will to accept or reject this grace.

The turning point in the life of people begins when they acknowledge their sin. Repentance of sin always precedes the conversion experience. Repentance means to be aware of self, to know who and what we are, and then to have an earnest desire to accept God's offer of relationship, to leave our present condition, and to enter the kingdom of God. Salvation comes through faith in Jesus Christ. Faith is complete trust in and loyalty to the kingdom of God as it is revealed in Jesus. The process of salvation may be sudden and dramatic or gradual and cumulative. It marks a new beginning that is possible through the atoning death of Jesus. The fact that Jesus was the sacrificial Lamb opens the door for us to be the recipients of God's justifying grace. Salvation is God's gift to us through Jesus Christ's death and resurrection. Through our faith in Christ, we receive God's justifying grace. Justification is not an arrived-at state but a moment-by-moment relationship of faith in Christ.

God's saving work then continues through sanctifying grace. This is the work of God within us that continues throughout life, shaping us, moving us toward perfection. This does not mean that we are perfect in the same way that a work of art or music might be considered perfect. It means that people are open to God's perfect love to flow into them and to flow out to others in servant ministry.

Back now to the question, How do we get in tune? We do so by God's grace through faith in Jesus Christ, the one who is worthy to open the seals of the will of God. Ask: *What would you write in your own summary of the message of hope found in Revelation 5:1-10?*

To close the session, ask: *Who is Jesus to you?* Then sing or pray in unison "O Jesus, I Have Promised."

[1] Information in "Bible Background" drawn from *The Revelation of John*, Volume 1, by William Barclay (The Westminster Press, 1976); pages 165–78.

TRY ANOTHER METHOD

■ Included in the Bible passage is the New Song sung to Christ by the four creatures and the twenty-four elders. Ask a member of the class to compose a new song, or poem, to present to the class members based on the message of hope in Revelation 5:1-10.

Invite two people to give a witness as to who Christ is in their life.

Paul was accused of "turning the world upside down." Ask: *What Christian teachings are "turning the world upside down" today?* (*Love is greater than military might. God has no favorites. Social status makes no difference in the Kingdom. God is with us.*)

Chapter Six

PROVISION FOR THE REDEEMED

PURPOSE

To emphasize the compassionate care God bestows on those who respond positively to his love

BIBLE PASSAGE

Revelation 7:1-3, 9-10, 13-17
Background: Revelation 7

> ### CORE VERSE
> The Lamb at the center of the throne will be their shepherd,
> and he will guide them to springs of the water of life,
> and God will wipe away every tear from their eyes.
>
> (Revelation 7:17)

GET READY

■ A meaningful worship center for this session would include a white cloth, a dirty cloth, and a cross or chalice.

On a chalkboard or on a large piece of paper, write the contrast of the two visions (see below). Also, write the definition of the word *righteousness* (see below).

BIBLE BACKGROUND

■ In the Book of Revelation, between the opening of the sixth and seventh seals of the scroll containing God's will, an interlude of two visions (Revelation 7:1-8 and 7:9-17) assures God's people of their security from the plagues and judgments to come. John is seeing the vision of the terrible last days and in particular the great tribulation such as has not been seen since the beginning of time. This will be the time of the final assault by all the forces of evil and the final devastation of the earth.

Revelation 7:1. As Chapter 7 opens, four angels are "standing at the four corners of the earth, holding back the four winds." John is seeing the world as it was conceived to be in the first century—flat and shaped in a square or rectangle with four corners. People believed that all the forces of nature were under the charge of angels. Therefore, these angels were doing their job of holding back the winds. The winds that came from due north, south, east, and west were considered favorable winds; but those that blew diagonally across the earth were viewed as quite harmful. The angels were holding back such diagonal winds from the corners of the earth.

Verses 2-3. An angel with a seal comes rising from the east. Coming from the east can have two significant meanings: (1) The sun, giver of life to the earth, rises in the east. The angel may represent the light and life of God that are present even when death and devastation are abroad. (2) John may be remembering the birth story of Jesus when the wise men from the east came to Palestine searching for the king, saying, "We observed his star at its rising" (Matthew 2:2b). It was natural for the angel to come from the same direction as the star that announced the birth of Jesus.

The angel has "the seal of the living God." The phrase "living God" is in contrast to gods made from stone, metal, or wood. These heathen gods are dead, not living, and were created by humans. In contrast, the living God is alive and involved in the life of the universe.

A second use of the phrase "living God" is to communicate to the faithful that they belong to and can relate to the living God. In this relationship they have the gifts of fellowship, power, help, and the eternal presence of the One who is alive.

The angel from the east holds the seal of the living God. Those who are to be brought safely through the ordeal are to be marked on their foreheads with this seal (Ezekiel 9:3b-4). The idea of the seal would have been familiar to people of the ancient Near East. Eastern kings wore a signet ring whose seal was used to authenticate documents. Merchants used a seal to indicate ownership. The makers of wine placed a seal on the jars of wine to identify their source of origin and to guarantee their quality. We see then that bearing the seal of the living God would mean belonging to God and being under God's power and authority.

In the early church this picture of sealings was specifically associated with two things. The first was baptism. Baptism was called "sealing" by some early church writers. It is as if God put a mark on people when they were baptized to show that they belonged to God. A wonderful story is told about a pastor who was trying to explain what happens when an infant is baptized. To illustrate, he told about a dairy that put its milk in glass bottles. Stamped on the bottom of each bottle were the words, "Property of Morning Star Dairy. If any other label, it is stolen." When we are baptized, we bear the seal of God. We are Christians. If we have any other label, we have been stolen from God.

The second use of "seal" in the early church was to be sealed with the gift of the Holy Spirit. Paul regularly used it in this way: "In him you also, when you had heard the word of truth, the gospel of your salvation, and had believed in him, were marked with the seal of the promised Holy Spirit" (Ephesians 1:13). This seal signified that the power and wisdom of God were released into the life of the person.

The student book adds a third concept of sealing. The writer says that the seal of the living God seems to be specifically related to the persecution of the Christians by Rome: "It is not so much a reward for being faithful as it is a measure of the compassionate care that God lavishes on his people when they are put in danger of their lives for the faith." Sealing,

then, is the mark of a loving God who is with them in the tribulation.

Verse 9. Here we move to a description of a gathering of the faithful. The multitude present is so great that no one can count them. They are from the whole world and are standing before the throne and before the Lamb. In this scene we find encouragement. Even though there will be pain, suffering, and death in the ordeal on earth, that is not the end. Look at what is ahead—being with the faithful of all generations in the presence of the Lamb of God, who made it all possible.

The faithful will wear white robes, a symbol of victory. They do not appear weary, battered, and defeated; they are gloriously dressed and are holding the victor's symbol, the palm branch.

Verse 10. The great multitude ascribes salvation to God and to the Lamb. It was God and Christ who brought them through the great ordeal. They were not protected from the experience, but in the experience they were victors. They were not saved from trouble, but they were triumphant in trouble. Through this time they were sustained in hope because of the glory awaiting them.

Looking at the strange contrast between the two visions will be helpful. (List these contrasts on a chalkboard or on a large piece of paper.) In the first vision, the group can be counted; there are 144,000 (7:4). In the second vision, they are an incalculably large number. In the first vision, the people come from the twelve tribes of Israel. In the second vision, the people come from every nation. In the first vision, the people are being prepared for imminent peril. In the second vision, their situation is victorious and secure. The first vision is to challenge the people to faithfulness and to assure them of God's love, care, and presence in the time of trial. The second vision is intended to bring encouragement to the believers by revealing what is awaiting them in heaven.

Verse 13. One of the elders asks John the identity of those dressed in white robes and where they came from. White robes were an understandable image in the ancient world, for it was forbidden to approach a pagan god in a soiled robe. In the Christian church people being baptized often wore white robes to symbolize the new life, whereas a dirty robe expressed in a symbolic way the breaking of baptismal vows.

In the vision the blessed ones' white robes also signify purity; for they have been cleansed from past sin, from the possible infection of sin in the present, and from the possible attack of sin in the future. The white robe also indicates victory that has come through the blood of the Lamb.

Verse 14. Here we discover who the multitude is—the faithful ones from all over the world who have come through the great ordeal, who "have washed their robes and made them white in the blood of the Lamb."

The phrase "blood of the Lamb" needs to be understood in the context of the first century, for the New Testament uses this image often. When twenty-first-century Americans think of blood, we usually think of death. To the Hebrews blood also meant life, for it is blood that gives life to the body. Therefore, when the New Testament speaks of the blood of Jesus Christ, it means the whole experience of his life and death—all that he did for us. We find this concept in the following passages (You may want to ask class members to read these passages aloud, or you may prefer to write them on a chalkboard or on a large piece of paper.):

(1) "whom God put forward as a sacrifice of atonement by his blood, effective through faith" (Romans 3:25)

(2) "much more surely then, now that we have been justified, by his blood" (Romans 5:9)

(3) "In him we have redemption through his blood" (Ephesians 1:7).

(4) "For in him all the fullness of God was pleased to dwell, and through him God was pleased to reconcile to himself all things . . . by making peace through the blood of his cross" (Colossians 1:19-20).

(5) "You know that you were ransomed from the futile ways inherited from your ancestors, not with perishable things like silver or gold, but with the precious blood of Christ, like that of a lamb without defect or blemish" (1 Peter 1:18-19).

(6) "If we walk in the light as he himself is in the light, we have fellowship with one another, and the blood of Jesus his Son cleanses us from all sin" (1 John 1:7).

Why so many references? Understanding the concept of the blood of Christ as including all aspects of his life shows the commitment of Christ to a total life of self-sacrifice.

Verse 15. What a revolutionary idea is presented here. The multitude, which consists of every race, tribe, people, and language, is before the throne of God. In the earthly Temple this could not happen. No Gentile could go beyond the Court of the Gentiles. An Israelite could enter the Court of the Israelites but could go no farther; no one could enter the Court of the Priests but the priests. In the heavenly temple there are no barriers; racial, class, gender, and age distinctions exist no more. In other words, the way into the very presence of God is open to every faithful soul.

The multitude will be in worship night and day. There need be no fear of anything anymore, for God will shelter them.

Verses 16-17. These verses have given comfort and hope to countless people. They include the spiritual promise of the ultimate satisfying of the hunger and thirst of the soul. This *promise* is also found elsewhere in the New Testament. Jesus said,

"I am the bread of life. Whoever comes to me will never be hungry, and whoever believes in me will never be thirsty" (John 6:35).
"Blessed are those who hunger and thirst for righteousness, for they will be filled" (Matthew 5:6). (Write the definition of righteousness on a chalkboard or on a large piece of paper: "Rightly related to God, to self, to others.")
"Let anyone who is thirsty come to me, and let the one who believes in me drink" (John 7:37-38).

Heaven will be a relationship in which there is no hunger or thirst or the heat of the scorching sun to burn tortured bodies. Christ is the answer to the world's hunger, thirst, pain, and sorrow. The Lamb will be the shepherd.

Shepherd is an image used in both the Old Testament and the New Testament. "The LORD is my shepherd" is the opening statement of the best loved of the Psalms (Psalm 23:1). Jesus said of himself, "I am the good shepherd" (John 10:11, 14). Shepherd, of course, was a meaningful image for anyone who lived in Palestine. The shepherd found still water for his sheep; he watched the flock carefully to prevent the sheep from falling from the rocky cliffs; the watchful eye of the shepherd saw a sheep that was "cast down" (on its back and unable to get up). In the vision we see the Divine Shepherd leading the multitude to springs of water without which there can be no life and where both body and soul are cared for.[1]

INTRODUCE OUR NEED

■ I wish that I could share with you a painting of Jesus Christ I own. It is most unusual; for when you look at it from a distance, you clearly see the head of Jesus with a crown of thorns piercing his brow. But as you move toward the painting, you are amazed to see that it is made up of the faces of people from all over the world—Asians, Native Americans, Africans, Caucasians. Some faces you immediately recognize, such as Mahatma Gandhi; Martin Luther King, Jr.; Jonas

Salk; and Mother Teresa. The others are people whose faces came from the mind of the artist—men, women, children, anybody, without rhyme or reason.

This painting is the work of William Zlinak, a professional artist. The inspiration for it came to him as a gift from God at a time when he cried out in desperation to God over the way he had lived and was living his life. At that instant a flash of light filled the room and for a split second Jesus' face appeared on the canvas. Zlinak picked up his brushes and began to paint. Fifteen hours later, he stepped back from the canvas for his first overall look. At that moment he was overwhelmed. All he could say was, "My God, did I do that?"

This painting reminds me of the vision of the great multitude that no one could count, "from every nation, from all tribes and peoples and languages" (Revelation 7:9). It is impossible to count the faces in the painting because every time you look, you see additional ones. The picture is a microcosm of the world's people.

What do the visions in Revelation 7 say? They say that God calls us to add our face to the face of Jesus Christ in order that the world may see the full nature of Christ in all his glory. It takes all of us to complete the face. When we are faithful to this call, we experience abundant living now, regardless of the outward circumstances of our life. The future is also assured; we will become part of the incalculable multitude dressed in white robes and holding palm branches as we worship God. What a message to a world that is so hungry and thirsty for meaning! Ask: *Have I given my face to be a part of Jesus Christ's face in order that the full nature of Christ can be visible in the world?*

LESSON PLAN

■ I was on a plane going to Tulsa, Oklahoma, where I was to speak the following day. Seated next to me was a young man about eighteen or nineteen years of age. When I asked where he was going, he replied, "San Antonio." He said his parents were divorced, and he had been living in New York with his father. His father was to be married soon and felt it best that his son live with his mother in San Antonio. This meant the young man had to leave high school a few weeks prior to the time he would graduate. He had checked with the school system in San Antonio, and there was no way he could enter there and complete his senior year. It would have to be completed in summer school or during the fall semester. As we talked about some life

options, the young man said in a voice filled with pain and want, "I need somebody in my corner!"

Such was the cry of the people to whom Revelation was originally written. They were being hit from all sides with poverty, persecution, low status, heathen gods, contempt, and negative cultural judgments. God's people needed a message of hope, of promise, of comfort to assure them Someone was in their corner. God gave this message in the form of a vision to John. God's people are to be marked by the seal of the living God; they belong to God, are claimed by God. In other words, God is in their corner.

The student book states that at times we all are faced with great distress and need to experience the seal of the living God. At those times a sufficient measure of God's grace is given to us, and we enter into a new plane of existence. This grace is not given to us because of our great accomplishments but because of our great need. Ask the following question from page 51 in the student book: *"Have you known people who have had an experience like sealing, or have you had such an experience yourself? If so, what were the circumstances?"* (*You might add to the answers the class members give the story of John Wesley , founder of Methodism, leaving the colony of Georgia feeling like a failure. Through this time of tribulation he was open to new insights and understandings from God, the Moravians, and friends in England. All this became a part of the journey that culminated at a house on Aldersgate Street when Wesley said, "I felt my heart strangely warmed," a time of sealing by the living God.*) Ask: *Is the seal of the living God on our church? What makes you think it is or is not?*

In response to the beautiful and meaningful poem in Revelation 7:15-17, the student book suggests that these words make clearer the nature of God's provision. The four images discussed are:

(1) When God is triumphant, there will no longer be hunger and thirst. Ask: *When we talk about hunger and thirst, what does it mean to us?* (*Most of us do not know physical hunger and thirst. However, we have deep spiritual hungers and thirsts. This is evidenced through drug abuse, alcoholism, divorce, sexual abuse, teenage suicide, crime, and violence.*) *What do the words of John say to these issues?* (*The risen Christ knows our problems and our tribulations and cares about us as we experience them. He yearns to help us have the victory over them. No matter how far we have fallen, there is hope for new life in the present and in the future.*)

(2) God's provision is that the scorching heat and sun will not burn them anymore. The student book says that heat saps physical and spiritual energy and creates discomfort. Ask: *What is the scorching spiritual*

heat we experience that robs us of energy and creates discomfort? (*The class members may suggest many other things; but certainly racism, joblessness, brokenness of life, and feelings of hopelessness and powerlessness rob us of energy and create discomfort.*)

(3) God's provision for his people is that the Lamb will become the Shepherd. In America the shepherd drives the sheep; in Palestine the shepherd leads the sheep. The reference to the shepherd, then, is to one who goes before us; our responsibility is to follow. Following is difficult for Americans because our culture places a great emphasis on leadership, not on "followship." However, the Shepherd is with us now and will lead us through trials and terrors if we will follow. We are never alone. The question then becomes, "Who am I following?" The answer determines life in the present and in the future.

(4) God's provision is that we will have access to "springs of the water of life" (Revelation 7:17). The "water of life" is spiritual (John 4:1-15). Ask: ***What are examples of spiritual thirst?*** (*Some examples are wanting to belong, having low self-esteem, feeling lonely, not feeling worthy or needed.*) These thirsts can be quenched by the living water that brings new life now and in the future.

(5) God's provision is that our tears will end. On this earth Christians shed tears over conditions that create poverty, crime, unwanted children, broken homes, and so forth. We cry because we love. If we do not love, we do not care about these conditions. God's promise is that in the present God is with us in our tears, but one day the conditions that caused these tears will be no more.

Ask: ***"Which of the provisions God has made for his people means the most to you?"*** [student book; page 53].

The vision of the multitude dressed in white robes has great meaning for us as well. These were the people who, during their earthly lives, had washed their robes in the blood of the Lamb and become pure in heart. The word *pure* means unmixed or unadulterated. Having a pure heart is a state of living in which life is centered and motives and acts are in agreement. That is, the heart is pure and the actions are pure. Jesus laid out the way to have such a life when he instructed us to "strive first for the kingdom of God and his right-

eousness, and all these things will be given to you" (Matthew 6:33). When we have mixed motives, we are not faithful anywhere and life is chaos.

Notice that those who were pure in heart had washed their robes in the blood of the Lamb (the whole life of Jesus Christ). This washing indicates a cooperative effort between people and Christ. We have the free will to remain adulterated or to have a pure heart. To live focused, with a pure heart, demands from us the most exacting self-examination. Some of the questions we need to ask ourselves daily are: *Is my prayer life a time of openness to God or just an exercise to say I have prayed? When I am in a service of worship, do I worship or am I there out of habit? When I am with friends and family, am I loving as Christ loves? Is the work I do in church done for Christ or to build up my own prestige?* To examine our own motives is difficult, for there are very few things that we do with unmixed motives. But, in bringing our dirty robes (adulterated lives) to Christ, he gives us the white robe. Thanks be to God!

To close the session, lead the class members in singing "Christ for the World We Sing."

[1]Information in "Bible Background" drawn from *The Revelation of John,* Volume 2, by William Barclay (The Westminster Press, 1976); pages 21–39.

TRY ANOTHER METHOD

■ Form small groups of three or four persons. Ask them to discuss the following topic: In Jesus Christ we meet a God who loves the world.

Invite someone to share what it means to have a pure heart in the everydayness of living.

Class members may wish to discuss the identity of the 144,000 sealed persons mentioned in Revelation 7:4. List the qualifications of this group described in Revelation 14:1-5. Ask: ***Could enough people be found anywhere to fill this quota? Why or why not?*** Note that most scholars agree the number 144,000 is an apocalyptic way of saying completeness; not one of the redeemed is missing.

Chapter Seven

THE VICTORIOUS CHRIST

PURPOSE

To help us grow in our understanding of the victorious lordship of Jesus Christ

BIBLE PASSAGE

Revelation 19:11-16; 20:11-15
Background: Revelation 19–20

> **CORE VERSE**
> On [the rider's] robe and on his thigh he has a name inscribed, "King of kings and Lord of lords."
> (Revelation 19:16)

GET READY

■ As you pray this week, ask God to use the lesson to help class members experience victory in any area of life they have not surrendered to the victorious Christ.

The student book gives an excellent and provocative description of what difference it will really make when Christ is Lord of all [see "Realms of the Kingdom"; pages 61–62]. Consider asking three class members who are good readers to read this section aloud, a paragraph at a time.

Have a chalkboard and chalk or a large piece of paper and markers available. As members enter your class setting, ask each to record a victory he or she has experienced this week.

BIBLE BACKGROUND

■ I do not know the name of the painting or the name of the artist, but the painting should be called *The Victorious Christ.* In this painting we see the world, a large globe with the nations carefully delineated. Standing on top of the world is Jesus Christ, dressed in a white robe, with arms outstretched as if encompassing the world. The nail prints are clearly visible in his hands and feet. This painting reminds me of the passage of Scripture we will be studying in this lesson, for it portrays the victorious Christ who through his selfless life and death became Lord of the universe. In this lesson we will be looking at one of the most dramatic events described in the Book of Revelation, the emergence of the conquering Christ.

Revelation 19:11. Heaven opens, and a rider on a white horse appears. The white horse is the symbol of the conqueror because it was on a white horse that a Roman general rode when he returned from a victorious military campaign. The rider is called "Faithful and True," two quite important words. "Faithful" means one who can be trusted absolutely. The rider of the white horse is one to whom complete loyalty can be given without any fear of betrayal. The other name is "True," in the sense that Jesus Christ is the one who brings the truth to humankind. This name also means genuine. Jesus is real, and in him we meet God's reality.

The rider of the white horse judges and makes war in righteousness. John finds his imagery in the Old Testament where it is said of God's chosen king,

He shall not judge by what his eyes see,
  or decide by what his ears hear;
 but with righteousness he shall judge the poor,
  and decide with equity for the meek of the
   earth. . . .

Righteousness shall be the belt around his waist,
and faithfulness the belt around his loins.

(Isaiah 11:3b-5)

The people of John's era knew about the perversion of justice. Wars were fought for selfish ambition and power, not for justice. Bribery of Roman officials was rampant. There was no equality in the court system; decisions were given by greedy judges.

The rider on a white horse holds great hope for the ones who have been oppressed. When the conquering Christ comes, his power will be exercised in righteousness.

Verse 12. Here we have a description of the conquering Christ. "His eyes are like a flame of fire." We have seen this description previously in the message to the church at Thyatira. It stands for the consuming power of Christ. "On his head are many diadems [royal crowns]." It may seem strange to us to learn that he wore many crowns, but it did not seem strange in John's day. It was not a bit unusual for a king to wear many crowns, signifying that he ruled over several areas. Christ is wearing many crowns to indicate that he is ruler over all the earth.

The next phrase, "and he has a name inscribed that no one knows but himself," is still a mystery. Several theories have been proposed as to its meaning; but as yet, no one is certain which, if any, is correct:

(1) Some people say the name is *Lord*. This suggestion is based on Philippians 2:9-11, where we read,

Therefore God also highly exalted him
and gave him the name that is above every
name,
so that at the name of Jesus
every knee should bend,
in heaven and on earth and under the earth,
and every tongue should confess that Jesus Christ
is Lord.

(2) Other people have suggested that the name is *YHWH,* the Jewish name for God; but the name was so holy that it was seldom pronounced. Instead, the people used the Hebrew word *Adonai,* which means Lord.

(3) Another theory affirms the Jewish belief that no person can know the name of God until he or she has entered heaven.

(4) Yet another theory is based on the ancient belief that to know the name of a divine being is to have power over him or her. Remember that in the story of the wrestling of Jacob with God, the divine being refused to give his name (Genesis 32:24-29).

Verse 13. Here we have two pictures of the warrior Christ. "He is clothed in a robe dipped in blood." Note that it is not his blood but that of his enemies. This is an entirely different picture from a "Lamb standing as if it had been slaughtered" (5:6). The important thing to remember in this vision is that the heavenly leader this time is the slayer, not the slain one. The vision reveals an eternal truth: Christ is the victor over evil.

The second warrior image is, "His name is called The Word of God." To a Jew a word was not merely a sound, it was powerful energy. Once it was spoken, it caused action. We see this concept at work in the story of Creation. Again and again we read, "God said," with action following (Genesis 1:3, 6-7, 9, 14-15, 24, 26-27). When John calls the warrior Christ "The Word of God," he means that all God said is alive and active in Christ.

Verses 14-15. Following the warrior Christ are the armies of heaven. Instead of wearing battle armor, they have on fine linen, white and pure; and they too are riding white horses. This scene brings to mind a statement Jesus made at the time of his arrest. When Peter cut off the ear of the slave of the high priest, Jesus said, "Put your sword back into its place; for all who take the sword will perish by the sword. Do you think that I cannot appeal to my Father, and he will at once send me more than twelve legions of angels?" (Matthew 26:52-53). We see the legions in this vision. This is a picture of the triumph of righteousness over evil. The faithful in Christ are part of the army of destruction.

As in the initial heavenly vision (Revelation 1:16), the warrior Christ has a sharp sword coming from his mouth "with which to strike down the nations" (19:15). The sword is his word, God's word. This is his only battle armament. By it and by it alone Christ brings the victory. The ultimate triumph is described with the statement, "He will rule them with a rod of iron; he will tread the wine press of the fury of the wrath of God the Almighty" (19:15).

Verse 16. Christ has another title that is visible for people to see as he rides by—"King of kings and Lord of lords." This title singles him out as the greatest of all rulers, the universal King and Lord of all.

Revelation 20:11. We now come to the Final Judgment. God, who is seated on a great white throne, is the Judge. We need to look at this image because there are many references to Christ being the Judge (Matthew 25:31-46; John 5:22-23; Acts 17:31; 2 Timothy 4:1). Why is it that sometimes God is the Judge and at other times Jesus is?

This question has two possible answers. The first

relates to the unity of the Father and the Son. Paul says Christ is the visible expression of the invisible God (Colossians 1:15). Paul also wrote, "For in him [Christ] all the fullness of God was pleased to dwell" (Colossians 1:19). Jesus said of himself, "The Father and I are one" (John 10:30). Therefore, the unity of the Father and the Son is such that there is no difficulty in ascribing the work of one to the other.

Second, God may be the Judge in Revelation because it is a book with deep Jewish roots. To a Jew, God is always unique. The foundation Scripture for all Jews is, "Hear, O Israel: The LORD is our God, the LORD alone. You shall love the LORD your God with all your heart, and with all your soul, and with all your might" (Deuteronomy 6:4). Loyalty to God as Judge would be natural to a Jew.

As the vision continues, the Judgment begins with the earth and heaven falling away. John may be thinking of familiar Old Testament passages that depict such an idea; for example,

> Lift up your eyes to the heavens,
>   and look at the earth beneath;
> for the heavens will vanish like smoke,
>   the earth will wear out like a garment.
> (Isaiah 51:6)

It seems that the presence of God is so awesome that there is no need for earth and heaven. In addition, the final Judgment clears the way for the new heaven and the new earth.

Verse 12. The Judgment begins. First, all the dead, regardless of status, race, gender, or economic resources, stand before the throne. The judgment of God is for all; no one is exempt. Books are opened. Two kinds are mentioned. The first contains a record of all the deeds of each one who stands before the throne of God. The idea is that God keeps a record of all the things people do. In other words, all through life we write our own destiny. In the Last Judgment it is not so much that God judges as it is that we are held responsible for what is written in the book.

Another book is "the book of life." Here the names of the righteous are recorded. These are persons who have not worshiped the beast (Rome) by taking part in the state cult. They have not paid tribute to the emperor as a god. In Revelation "the book of life" is mentioned six times (3:5; 13:5-8; 17:8; 20:12, 15; 21:27).

"The book of life" was a familiar title to people in John's day. Every ruler had a roll book of the people who were under his control. When a person died, his or her name was removed from the roll. To have your name in the book of life meant you were alive.

Verse 13. It is said that at the time of Judgment, the sea will give up its dead. In the ancient world this was very important; burial was essential. People believed that otherwise the person's spirit had no resting place and would wander, having no home either in heaven or on earth. Those who died at sea had had no burial. This is also a way of saying that those who have died accidentally will also appear before the Judge; no one will escape punishment or reward.

Verse 14. The two great enemies of humankind, "Death and Hades," are destroyed after giving up their dead. Their destruction comes through being thrown into the lake of fire, which is identified as the second death. The second death is a reference to spiritual death, total separation from God.

Verse 15. The last verse in Chapter 20 has a strong sense of finality. It is a verse that issues a clarion call for the evangelization of all people as well as for individual discernment. Those whose names are not found in the book of life will experience the lake of fire. What we do on earth is of the utmost importance, for we are writing our final destiny.[1]

INTRODUCE OUR NEED

■ Leslie Weatherhead told about being in Royal Albert Hall in London with his father-in-law, whom he described as a saint. The program for the evening was Handel's "Messiah," featuring the London Symphony. Dr. Weatherhead said all the people in the audience were standing as the "Hallelujah Chorus" was being sung in all its beauty and glory. When the choir came to the words "King of kings and Lord of lords," Dr. Weatherhead said he felt a jab in his ribs. He turned to see his father-in-law with tears streaming down his face. In a voice filled with great emotion, the father-in-law said, "Leslie, Leslie, he is King of kings and Lord of lords; but that's my Jesus they are singing about."

In the Book of Revelation we see Jesus Christ in both roles. He is the Lamb, the atonement for the sins of each human being. He is truly "my Jesus," for he loves and cares for us as individuals. And he is the victorious Christ, the one who will eventually command the forces of good and destroy evil as the King of kings and Lord of lords.

Ask the following question from page 61 in the student book: *"What modern illustration could you use to express the majesty and power of Christ in victory?"* (*Some class members will point out that the very existence of the church illustrates the power of the risen Christ. Others will mention the presence of Christ in the lives of people and the power of Christ assisting us in difficult times. Some members will point out the evidence that evil does not win, that they are aware of the power of Christ wherever and whenever they see the demise of racism, poverty, hatred, greed, selfishness, and so forth.)*

Then ask: ***What difference does it make in your life to know that Christ is and will be victorious?***

LESSON PLAN

■ In the ancient world the word *lord* meant the one in charge. The lord had complete power over the life of the nation and the people who lived therein. In the visions of the victorious Christ, he is seen as the Lord of the universe. Paul puts it this way: "He is the image of the invisible God, the firstborn of all creation; for in him all things in heaven and on earth were created . . .—all things have been created through him and for him. He himself is before all things, and in him all things hold together" (Colossians 1:15-17).

We live in a world that was created for, through, and in Christ Jesus, a world that Christ holds together. When Jesus is Lord, life is as it is meant to be. [If three class members are prepared to read the student book section "Realms of the Kingdom," pages 61–62, ask them to do so at this point.] When Jesus is not Lord, life is at cross purposes with itself and chaos results. If we try to run the universe on any other principle than that revealed in the life and teachings of Jesus, it will not work; the world will be on a collision course.

The amazing teaching of the New Testament is that the victorious Christ comes and lives in the hearts of human beings. For an individual to say, "Jesus is Lord" is to respond to God's saving grace made possible in Christ. When Jesus is Lord, he is in charge of all of life as lived out in daily relationships. The student book points out that confusion at times surrounds the idea of the lordship of Christ, that people want it "to relate only to their own pet projects or peeves" [page 57]. To hold this idea is self-destructive, for life has meaning only if it is totally under the lordship of Christ. Such a relationship is never partial; it is total, or it does not exist at all.

Say: ***The student book gives several definitions of the phrase "Jesus is Lord." (See pages 56–57.) What do these words mean to you?***

A comparison of two biblical images of the Last Judgment would be helpful at this point in the session. We have already seen in the white throne judgment scene in Revelation how "the book of deeds" and "the book of life" are written records of what a person ha[s] done on earth. What is written in these books deter[-]mines one's eternal destiny.

Matthew 25:31-46 includes a similar image. As in th[e] Book of Revelation, all nations are gathered together[;] they will be separated as a shepherd separates hi[s] sheep from his goats. All who were listening to Jesu[s] tell this parable knew that a good shepherd always sep[-]arated sheep from goats; doing so was a caring act[.] Goats like to sleep where there is some kind of shelter[;] sheep like to sleep outdoors.

The Son of Man then says to those on his right hand[,] "Come, you that are blessed by my Father, inherit th[e] kingdom prepared for you from the foundation o[f] the world; for I was hungry and you gave me food[,] I was thirsty and you gave me something to drink, I wa[s] a stranger and you welcomed me, I was naked and yo[u] gave me clothing, I was sick and you took care of me[,] I was in prison and you visited me" (Matthew 25:34-36)[.] Notice what the works of the righteous are—a lifestyl[e] of loving service, of meeting human needs whereve[r] they are, of being for others what Christ would be.

The people of the ancient Near East never though[t] one dimensionally about life; they thought four dimen[-]sionally. When words like *hungry, thirsty, naked, stranger* and *sick* were used, they included not only the physica[l] but also the mental, spiritual, and relational aspects o[f] the conditions these words described. To say, "I wa[s] hungry and you gave me food" meant a feeding of th[e] spirit, the mind, the body, and relationships. Thi[s] would be true in each area mentioned in the parable[.] The student book draws on the Book of James' teach[-]ings concerning faith and works when it states that "it i[s] not a matter of faith or works but of works of faith. W[e] could add that it is not a matter of love or works but o[f] works of love. The whole of the person is to becom[e] a part of the whole victory in Christ" [page 59].

What follows next in the parable is most interesting[.] Those who are invited to come into the Kingdom ar[e] amazed. They had no idea they had done good work[s] for Jesus. The acts they had been doing were just thei[r] way of living; they did not do them in an attempt to ge[t] into the Kingdom. In other words, when faith is cen[-]tered in Christ, acts of love become the norm.

As we continue in the parable, we hear Jesus explai[n] what the universal standard of judgment is: "Truly I tel[l] you, just as you did it to one of the least of these who ar[e] members of my family, you did it to me" (Matthew 25:40)[.] Notice the word *least*. Jesus is saying that the universa[l] standard of judgment is based on how you have loved th[e] ones who have needs and concerns that are overlooked[.]

in society. We know from this parable and from the Book of Revelation that acts of love to these people will open the way for entrance into the ultimate kingdom of God.

Those who did not see and serve the *least* are told, "You that are accursed, depart from me into the eternal fire prepared for the devil and his angels; for I was hungry and you gave me no food, I was thirsty and you gave me nothing to drink, I was a stranger and you did not welcome me, naked and you did not give me clothing, sick and in prison and you did not visit me" (Matthew 25:41-43). The response from this group is, "Lord, when was it that we saw you hungry or thirsty or a stranger or naked or sick or in prison, and did not take care of you?" (Matthew 25:44). Look carefully at what these people are saying: "We would have done these acts for you, Lord. We didn't see you in any of these conditions you are describing. If we had, we would have done these things for you." You cannot help but feel pain for this group. They have lived, but they have missed the whole purpose of life. Having the gift of life means assuming responsibility for performing acts of love that flow from faith in Christ. Ask: ***Do I see and serve the "least of these"? How does our church serve the least?***

What do we learn about the Last Judgment from these two accounts (Matthew 25:31-46; Revelation 20:11-15)?

(1) All people must face a day of accountability to God; no one is exempt.

(2) What we do on earth determines our ultimate destiny.

(3) God loves all people, and we as individual human beings are called to do the same.

(4) People have the ability and the resources to meet the needs of others.

(5) God is with us daily, cares for us, and knows us personally.

(6) God's standard of judgment is different from the world's standard. God's standard is, How deeply have you loved?

Close the session by singing as a prayer "Here I Am, Lord."

[1] Information in "Bible Background" drawn from *The Revelation of John*, Volume 2, by William Barclay (The Westminster Press, 1976); pages 179–84 and 194–97.

TRY ANOTHER METHOD

■ Invite someone to the session who is involved in humanitarian service to speak about his or her work with people.

Discuss the American standard of judgment as compared to Matthew 25:31-46. Or, compare contemporary society to the vision of the Kingdom found in the student book section "Realms of the Kingdom," pages 61–62.

Ask a talented singer to sing as a solo "Help Us Accept Each Other."

Chapter Eight

A NEW HEAVEN AND EARTH

PURPOSE

To help us celebrate the hope we have in Jesus Christ

BIBLE PASSAGE

Revelation 21:1-7, 22-27
Background: Revelation 21:1–22:5

> **CORE VERSE**
>
> I saw a new heaven and a new earth; for the first heaven and the first earth had passed away, and the sea was no more. (Revelation 21:1)

GET READY

■ What a message you have to share in this session—the promise of a new heaven and a new earth! The class setting should reflect this theme. Plan to have a new arrangement of seating. We tend to get settled in our "place" and stay there. Have symbols of new life on the walls, on the worship center, and on the seats. These symbols could be butterflies; empty egg shells; flowers; maps; pictures of rainbows, children, adults enjoying life; and so forth.

The student book discusses five deepest longings that are addressed in the Book of Revelation. These have been summarized in a list below. Prior to the session, copy the list on a chalkboard or on a large piece of paper.

BIBLE BACKGROUND

■ One Sunday a five-year-old boy was in worship with his parents. The pastor was paraphrasing God's response to Job. In a big booming voice he said, "Where were you when I created the stars? Where were you when I created the sea and gave it boundaries? Where were you when I commanded the sun to rise? Where were you when I created lions and mountain goats and gave might to horses?" The lad had been drawn into the message and could see through his imagination what the pastor was describing. He held back a response to the questions just as long as he could. Suddenly, he said in a loud voice, "I wasn't there; but thanks anyway, God!"

I feel like that child as we move into Chapter 21 of Revelation. The description of the new heaven and new earth touches every fiber of my being. I want to call out, "It hasn't come yet; but thanks anyway, God, for the assurance that it is to be!" Chapters 21 and 22 provide a magnificent climax for Revelation and for the Bible.

Revelation 21:1. The new heaven and the new earth have come. The word *new* here does not mean simply another earth and heaven but a new kind of heaven and a new kind of earth that are radically different from the old. This concept is developed in the verses that follow.

The first earth and the first heaven have passed away, and the sea is no more. In the time of John the sea was regarded as a symbol of turbulence and as the enemy of humankind. The Egyptians saw it as the power that swallowed up the waters of the Nile and left their fields without crops. In several places in the Bible the sea symbolizes power that God alone can control (Psalm 89:9; Isaiah 57:20). In addition, there was the human element: Most people feared the sea. Navigational equipment was limited at best. The sea held power and mystery that caused people to see it as evil. Having the sea no more would be welcomed.

Verse 2. Here we see that "the holy city," "the new Jerusalem," comes "down out of heaven from God, prepared as a bride adorned for her husband." This image embodies the long-held dream of the Jews for the restoration of Jerusalem, the Holy City. Old Testament references to the restoration are many (Isaiah 60:10-14; Ezekiel 48:30-35).

An element of the philosophical thought of Plato is also present in this imagery. His doctrine of ideas or forms held that in the invisible world there existed the perfect form or idea of everything on earth and that all things on earth were imperfect copies of heavenly realities. If this be so, there is in existence the heavenly Jerusalem of which the earthly Jerusalem is an imperfect copy. The writer of Hebrews apparently thought in these terms: "You have come to Mount Zion and to the city of the living God, the heavenly Jerusalem" (12:22). The "new Jerusalem," then, is the heavenly Jerusalem, the perfect form, that comes from God to replace the imperfect form. She is beautiful beyond description, "as a bride adorned for her husband" (Revelation 21:2).

Verses 3-4. The covenant God made with Israel is reflected in these verses: "I will place my dwelling in your midst, and I shall not abhor you. And I will walk among you, and will be your God, and you shall be my people" (Leviticus 26:11-12). We hear the same covenant words in Revelation 21:3: "The home of God is among mortals. / He will dwell with them; / they will be his peoples."

The New Jerusalem is the promise of having fellowship with God and receiving the love that comes from being at home with God. Tears, grief, death, crying, and pain are gone; for they are a part of the old order. Think about the vast number of people who have found great comfort and hope in these words. Ask: *What do these verses mean to you? What difference do they make in the everyday activities of living?*

Verse 5. For only the second time in the Book of Revelation (see 1:8), God speaks. God is the one who is making all things new. Again we are back among the dreams of the prophet. Isaiah heard God say, "I am about to do a new thing; / now it springs forth, do you not perceive it?" (43:19).

Paul, too, captured this dream in words: "So if anyone is in Christ, there is a new creation: everything old has passed away; see, everything has become new!" (2 Corinthians 5:17). God, the Creator, is now recreat-

ing. Although these words primarily refer to the final renewing, use of the present tense indicates that God is continually making things new. God speaks again, asking that these words be written; for they "are trustworthy and true" (Revelation 21:5). When something is written, it can be shared from person to person and from generation to generation. What is trustworthy, what is true, must be recorded, remembered, and relied upon.

Verse 6. Again God speaks: "It is done!" In the mind of the believer, all that God has promised is on the way now to complete fulfillment. No loose ends remain to be tied up; the final victory, the New Jerusalem, is to be. To reinforce this point, God says, "I am the Alpha and the Omega, the beginning and the end."

A promise is given to all who thirst: "I will give water as a gift from the spring of the water of life." This statement immediately brings to mind the words of Jesus to the woman at Jacob's well: "The water that I will give will become in them a spring of water gushing up to eternal life" (John 4:14b). Notice the use of the word *give* in both verses. Spiritual water cannot be bought; it needs only to be received, for it is a free gift from God and Christ. Ask: *If spiritual water is a free gift, why are there so many spiritually thirsty people?*

Verse 7. The New Jerusalem is not for everyone; it is only for those who are faithful and loyal to God, for those who have not been seduced to follow other gods but who in all circumstances give their allegiance to God. They are the ones who will receive the inheritance of God. The verse continues with the covenant words, "I will be their God and they will be my children." It is interesting that the word *children* is used. If you are someone's child, you belong to that person and the person belongs to you. You are a family, and families share resources with one another. This understanding adds additional meaning to the use of the word *inherit* in the verse. What a beautiful image to describe relationships in the New Jerusalem! God is in a covenant relationship with his children, sharing the family resources.

The student book gives special insight into this subject, mentioning that human beings want love more than they want anything else. The lesson describes how many of our activities are designed to gain the love we feel we do not get. The student book then says, "Yet in the greater scheme of things, love is a free gift of the gracious God who made us and continues to care for us. The vision of the last days is that there will no longer be any need to solicit love. The need will be satisfied before it is even recognized" [page 69].

Verse 22. In verses 9-21, John describes the New Jerusalem. The description is awesome, and John apparently wanted it that way so that in our minds we might be carried into the wonder of all that God is doing for his people. When we get to verse 22, John turns his attention to aspects of life within the New Jerusalem. Immediately, John describes a unique feature of this incredible city: There is no temple, for in essence the whole city is the temple. In verse 16, an angel measures the city: "Its length and width and height are equal." In other words, it is a perfect cube. This feature has great meaning, for in Solomon's Temple the Holy of Holies was a perfect cube (1 Kings 6:20). The symbolism John is attempting to convey is that all of the holy city is the Holy of Holies, the home of God. No temple is needed, for the whole city is filled with the presence of God.

Verse 23. The city has no need for light; God is the light. Everyone and everywhere is illuminated by God's glory. This concept has Old Testament roots as well. In Isaiah we read, "The sun shall no longer be your light by day, / nor for brightness shall the moon give light to you by night; / but the Lord will be your everlasting light" (60:19).

We can also testify to God being light to us now. Many times in the "dark night of the soul" and in the joys of life, God's light has given new life to us. God's light is visible in creation. A colleague of mine had become a grandmother for the first time. When she brought the picture of "the most beautiful grandchild in the world" for me to see, we both marveled at God's creation revealed in little ones. God's light is on earth where love, justice, and mercy are found.

Verse 24. In John's day this passage would be quite difficult for some people to accept, just as it is for many people today. The holy city is God's plan for all of humankind—not one nation or one ethnic group. It is filled with God's light and was created by One whose nature is love. Therefore, all nations are invited to live in the holy city. Ask: *How does our church reflect the nature of the holy city?*

Verse 25. In the ancient world cities had walls around them for protection. To enter or leave the city, people passed through large gates. These gates were closed at night for the safety of all within the walls. John tells us that in the holy city the gates will never be shut, conveying the sense of perfect freedom of access and fellowship with God for all. Notice these comforting words: "And there will be no night there." The ancient peoples, like some persons today, were afraid of the dark. In the holy city the fear of darkness will no longer exist; God's light has removed it.

Verse 26. Have you ever been to an International Fair? At the college where I taught, we had a large number of students from countries other than the United States. To celebrate their presence and to get to know about the nations they represented, we held an International Fair each year for the community and for the college. Each of the international students had a display from his or her country; they shared customs, music, and dance. All who attended felt a bonding with the students and learned much about other countries in the world family. In this verse we have a picture of an International Fair. People will bring to the holy city the glory and honor of all the nations. Visualize this scene—God's worldwide family with its rich diversity at home.

Verse 27. The chapter ends with an emphatic statement. Even though all people are invited to be inhabitants of the New Jerusalem, some will not be there. This is a choice given to people; this is not God's desire. Conditions have been given for participation in this great future; these requirements are clear and apply to all persons. Those who will not repent of the evil of their ways are barred from the city of God.

We often emphasize the love of God expressed through acceptance, forgiveness, and reconciliation. However, another facet of God's love also needs to be understood—the freedom to make our own decisions. We are not puppets in God's hands. The God whose nature is love has created us with the capacity to grow into the likeness of God's nature (sanctification), but we can say no to this opportunity. If we do say no, then our choices create consequences. John tells us that nothing unclean will enter the holy city, only those whose names are written in the Lamb's book of life. The choice is ours![1]

INTRODUCE OUR NEED

■ At the close of a day of study and classes, several theology students enjoyed going to the gym at a seminary to play basketball. They always found the janitor reading his Bible as he waited to close the gym for the night. Many times he would discuss verses with the seminarians, and a real friendship was established.

One evening the students found the janitor reading the Book of Revelation and saw that he was thoroughly enjoying its contents. This intrigued the students; so they asked, "Do you understand what you are reading?" Without a moment of hesitation the janitor eplied, "Yes, I understand it completely." Bewildered by his reply, they asked again, "Do you really understand this book?" Again, in complete confidence he said, "Yes!" Not believing anyone could be so knowledgeable, one of the students said, "Would you tell us what the Book of Revelation is all about?" With a hearty laugh the janitor replied, "It says Jesus wins."

The janitor was correct; Jesus wins! Even though there are visions, beasts, monsters, horrible battles, and frightening judgments, a powerful theme begins in Chapter 1 of the Book of Revelation and, like a single thread in a piece of cloth, weaves its way through to the closing chapter. Jesus Christ is God's Son. He is the One worthy to open the scroll that contains the will of God. This will is embodied in the sacrificial life of Jesus. The many enemies of God thought their mighty weapons of evil would put an end to Jesus, but love triumphed over evil. Jesus is the victorious Christ, and those who are faithful are also victorious. Even though we presently know some likeness of heaven on earth, at the time of the end there will be a holy city with open gates ready to receive those whose names are in the Lamb's book of life. Yes, Revelation does say, "Jesus wins."

Ask: *What does it mean in your life to know that love will triumph over evil?* After the class members have responded, ask the following question from page 68 in the student book: *"If you were describing the best of heaven and earth for a modern audience, what images would you use from today's world?"*

LESSON PLAN

First United Methodist Church in Waynesville, North Carolina, experienced a fire that destroyed the beautiful sanctuary. This tragic event did not stop worship, Sunday school, or other activities that made up the life of the congregation, however. A large sign was put up by the shell of the sanctuary that read, "A Burned-out Sanctuary but an Alive Congregation."

In the description of the New Jerusalem, the absence of a temple is at first startling; but as we read on, we realize that a temple or a sanctuary is not necessary for worship. The student book reminds us that, in a way, the absence of a temple in the New Jerusalem was a sign of the nature of worship for the early Christians. Jesus, in speaking to the woman at the well, said, "Woman, believe me, the hour is coming when you will worship the Father neither on this mountain nor in Jerusalem. . . . But the hour is coming, and is now here, when the true worshipers will worship the Father in spirit and truth" (John 4:21-23).

The New Jerusalem and First United Methodist Church teach us some key elements about worshiping God. It is no longer necessary to have any temple other than the heart itself. Wherever God is in residence, there is a temple. Ask: *"What is your idea of the most effective worship service?"* [student book; page 69].

The student book states that the Book of Revelation addresses some of the deepest longings of the human heart:

(1) the need to love and to be loved
(2) the need to feel that we belong to something greater than ourselves, something that will enhance and complete our own existence
(3) the need to be free of the pain of life
(4) the need to be our best selves
(5) the need to feel that the direction of our lives is the same as that of the universe

The Book of Revelation assures us that there will be a time when these longings will no longer be unmet needs but a lived reality in the New Jerusalem—a time of living in accordance with the will of God in the very presence of God. Ask: *"What are your own deepest needs? Which are being satisfied?"* [student book; page 72].

As you discuss these two questions, I feel sure it will be evident that the class members, like all human beings, have deep needs. We have been given assurance that in the New Jerusalem we will abide in the presence of God and with the people of God. But what news does the Book of Revelation bring us for the living of our lives today?

The first news is a theme that runs throughout the book: God is with us; we are not alone. In each of the letters to the seven churches, the assuring words of Christ are, "I know you; I know your problems and needs." A loving Creator does not abandon that which is created. Just as God is present in the holy city, God is with us now.

Second, the Book of Revelation gives us a perfect picture of what the church on earth is to be. The description of the New Jerusalem serves as a vivid and beautiful description of the church. The presence of God will fill the whole area. The light of God will dispel all darkness. People with tears will have them wiped away. Those who mourn will be comforted. The second death (spiritual death) will be no more. Those in pain will find healing.

The door of the church will always be open. The open door gives people the freedom to come, to worship, and to enjoy fellowship; but it also gives them the freedom to go forth and witness to God's amazing grace. The open door signifies that all people are welcome. Race, age, social position, economic status, and nationality are not important in the true church. Love, respect, and acceptance of all persons is the norm.

The church is actively involved in works of love. The works of many churches are now bringing transformation in human lives and communities. The following list does not begin to tell all:

Out of concern for abandoned persons with AIDS, a church bought a building where they could house these people and give them medical help, friendship, and loving care.

One church is in a multi-million-dollar building program. However, one tenth of the money received for building will be used for home and foreign missions.

Many churches believe a day care ministry for children is a number one priority.

Believing that God loves the inner city and its people, a church has made a commitment to be Christ's representative to every inch of the area.

Many churches have daily meals and gracious fellowship for the poor. Beds for sleep, showers for the body, job information, and friendship are provided by these churches.

Ask: **What can we add to this list that is being done b** **our church? by our class?**

Another magnificent insight that comes from th Book of Revelation is the reality that God loves all pec ple and all are called to be sons and daughters of Goc In a world fragmented, broken, and weary because o social, economic, political, religious, and racial cor flicts, the knowledge that all are loved equally an unconditionally is news almost too good to be true. I is the message the world's heart yearns to hear. We car not read Revelation without discovering the unfatl omable love of God for people.

In closing, lead the class members in the prayer a the end of the student book lesson.

[1]Information in "Bible Background" drawn from *The Revelation John,* Volume 2, by William Barclay (The Westminster Press, 1976 pages 199–206 and 215–19.

TRY ANOTHER METHOD

■ In light of the vision of the New Jerusalem in Reve lation 21:9-27, discuss Paul's statement, "For to me, li ing is Christ and dying is gain" (Philippians 1:21).

Discuss the following question: In light of our Bibl passage, what does it mean to pray, "Thy Kingdor come, thy will be done on earth"?